MODEL JURY INSTRUCTIONS

Patent
Litigation

SECTION OF LITIGATION
American Bar Association

The
MODEL JURY INSTRUCTIONS
Series

Business Torts Litigation

Construction Litigation

Employment Litigation

Patent Litigation

Securities Litigation

Defending Liberty
Pursuing Justice

SECTION OF LITIGATION
American Bar Association

MODEL JURY INSTRUCTIONS

Patent Litigation

Defending Liberty
Pursuing Justice

Cover design by ABA Publishing.

09 08 07 06 05   5 4 3 2 1

Library of Congress Cataloging-in-Publication Data

   Model jury instructions : patent litigation / Denise Loring, editor.—1st ed.
      p. cm.
   ISBN 1-59031-348-8
     1. Instructions to juries—United States—Forms. 2. Patent suits—United States—Forms. I. Loring, Denise, 1954–
   KF3155.M63   2005
   347.73'758—dc22

                                      200500167

Discounts are available for books ordered in bulk. Special consideration is given to state bars, CLE programs, and other bar-related organizations. Inquire at Book Publishing, American Bar Association, 750 North Lake Shore Drive, Chicago, Illinois 60611.

www.ababooks.org

Table of Contents

DRAFTING COMMITTEE

The following members of the American Bar Association, Section of Litigation, Committee on Intellectual Property Litigation participated in the preparation of these Model Jury Instructions for Patent Litigation:

The Honorable Avern Cohn
United States District Court for the Eastern District of
    Michigan
Detroit, Michigan

The Honorable Patti B. Saris
United States District Court for the District of
    Massachusetts
Boston, Massachusetts

The Honorable Ronald M. Whyte
United States District Court for the Northern District
    of California
San Jose, California

Morgan Chu, Esq.
Irell & Manella LLP
Los Angeles, California

Thomas L. Creel, Esq.
Kaye Scholer, LLP
New York, New York

Donald R. Harris, Esq.
Jenner & Block LLP
Chicago, Illinois

Robert T. Haslam, Esq.
Heller Ehrman White & McAuliffe, LLP
Menlo Park, California

John F. Lynch, Esq.
Howrey Simon Arnold & White, LLP
Houston, Texas

Denise L. Loring, Esq.
Fish & Neave LLP
New York, New York

Roderick R. McKelvie, Esq.
Fish & Neave LLP
Washington, D.C.

Joseph J. Richetti, Esq.
Bryan Cave LLP
New York, New York

Herbert F. Schwartz, Esq.
Fish & Neave LLP
New York, New York

Michael O. Warnecke, Esq.
Mayer, Brown, Rowe & Maw LLP
Chicago, Illinois

ACKNOWLEDGMENTS

The Model Jury Instructions for Patent Litigation were prepared through the combined efforts of the Committee and the Model Patent Jury Instruction Committee of the Federal Circuit Bar Association. The Federal Circuit Bar Association Committee members who participated are:

Mark J. Abate, Esq.
Morgan Finnegan LLP

Philip S. Beck, Esq.
Bartlit Beck Herman Palenchar & Scott LLP

Denise L. Loring, Esq.
Fish & Neave LLP

Robert C. Morgan, Esq.
Fish & Neave LLP

Matthew D. Powers, Esq.
Weil, Gotshal & Manges LLP

Joseph J. Richetti, Esq.
Bryan Cave LLP

Harry J. Roper, Esq.
Jenner & Block LLP

William C. Steffin, Esq.

Special thanks is given to Julie A. Blackman, PhD, who reviewed drafts and provided suggestions and comments on how to simplify the instructions and improve jury comprehension.

Denise L. Loring, Esq.
Fish & Neave LLP

Joseph J. Richetti, Esq.
Bryan Cave LLP

FOREWORD TO MODEL JURY INSTRUCTIONS SERIES

Jury instructions: that is where the rubber hits the road in the law. At their best, jury instructions summarize cogently, clearly, and distinctly the contours of the law that a jury must apply to the facts. At their worst, jury instructions are tangled, arcane, incomprehensible legalese masquerading as a guide for the jury.

The jury instructions in this volume pertain to patent law litigation. They are for those among us who, every once in a while, fail to settle a case and therefore must to trial. When a case is tried to a judge, that judge is presumed to know the law. When the case is tried to a jury of laypeople, they are presumed not to know the law. Therefore, they must be provided with a legal road map. These jury instructions are intended to serve that purpose. They can be used as such a guide not only in court before a jury, but also for evaluating and preparing a case for trial. These jury instructions are designed to tell a jury, and therefore you, what you must prove to prevail in your case. We hope you will find the guidance provided here enlightening and useful at the multiple stages of taking, preparing, and trying a case.

Each jury instruction is intended to be party-neutral. However, because ours is an adversary system of justice, lawyers may try to rewrite these neutral instructions in a manner that better presents the case for their clients. We wish those lawyers luck in convincing a court that the proposed reformulation conforms to the status of the law. Obviously, because the law is rarely static, the success of such reformulation will closely track any developments in the law.

In the notes that follow each instruction, you will find discussion of cases from which the instruction is derived, whether plaintiffs and defendants disagree on its use, and how it might be modified depending upon the individual circumstances.

These model jury instructions do not incorporate standard form instructions dealing with generalized burdens of proof, credibility of witnesses, or other such background matters that every set of jury instructions is presumed to include. The instructions here do include instructions on a wide range of issues and causes of action that arise in the context of patent law litigation. The table of contents spells these out for the reader and is intended to assure ease of use.

As the Section of Litigation of the American Bar Association, we can imagine few more useful tools to provide our colleagues than cogent, clear, and distinct jury instructions. We have designated these jury instructions as "model" ones because we hope that, in time, that is what they will become.

To that end, we invite the readers and users of these proposed model jury instructions to share their reactions with us. Let us know which of the instructions work and which do not. Let us know which of the instructions you believe could be more clearly written. Let us know which of the instructions a court has refused to give and why. In a second edition, we will try to incorporate your feedback so that these proposed "model" jury instructions in fact become model in use.

This volume is the fifth that the Section of Litigation has produced on jury instructions. The first volume is devoted to business torts. The second is devoted to employment law issues, and has been distributed to each of the federal trial judges. The third model jury instructions volume is devoted to securities litigation. The feedback from judicial and practitioner users has been positive indeed. We hope that this volume will be accorded the same acceptance received by the three prior jury instruction volumes. The profession certainly owes a large debt of gratitude to those individual lawyers who have given so unstintingly and so generously of their time to produce these jury instructions.

We hope that the five volumes of jury instructions now in print constitute a respectable body of work, but it is only a beginning. Other volumes are in the drafting or planning stages. In time, we plan to present model jury instructions for many other areas of the law that often form the underlying basis for cases tried in the federal courts.

Book Publishing Board
Section of Litigation

INTRODUCTION

In preparing these model patent jury instructions, we attempted to create a set of plain-English, party-neutral instructions that not only reflect the current state of the law, but are also simple and easy to understand. In furtherance of this goal, the instructions include concrete examples where appropriate. For example, we included an example of a table to illustrate how an invention may be claimed using the various types of patent claim limitations.

The instructions focus on the jury's role as fact-finder and the broad legal principles of patent law. They do not, however, address every factor or legal theory that courts have used to decide a particular issue. If such a factor or legal theory is relevant to a particular case, it may be addressed by a special instruction or through arguments made by trial counsel.

The instructions are divided into two parts: preliminary instructions and final instructions. Preliminary jury instructions are an important tool in aiding jurors to perform their fact-finding role. Jurors in civil trials are presented with enormous amounts of unfamiliar and often extremely complex information. This is especially true in patent cases, where jurors must grapple with a unique field of law and factual subject matter that often involves sophisticated technology.

Preliminary instructions provide the framework within which jurors may process and filter the information they receive. The preliminary instructions introduce to the jury the factual and legal framework within which the trial will take place, and explain what will be expected of them, all before they hear any evidence. This facilitates jury comprehension and retention of the information the jurors receive at trial.

The final instructions included here encompass the major issues that arise in patent litigation. Because every issue does not arise in every case, each instruction is designed to stand on its own, enabling the user to pick and choose the instructions relevant to his or her case. The instructions assume the more common situation in a patent infringement case, i.e., a suit in which the plaintiff is enforcing the patent(s)-in-suit against the accused infringer, but may be easily modified for use in declaratory judgment actions, where the plaintiff is accused of infringing the defendant's patent.

The final instructions include introductory sections and notes. The introductory sections provide an overview of the legal issues. The notes discuss current developments in patent law, and point out areas where potential conflicts exist in the case law.

Part I–Preliminary Instructions

Chapter One
Burdens of Proof

1. Burdens of Proof

In any legal action, facts must be proven by a specified standard, known as the "burden of proof." In a patent case, one of two different burdens of proof will be used, depending on the issue being decided.

The first burden of proof requires that, in order for a party to prevail, you must be persuaded that what the party seeks to prove is more probably true than not true.

The second burden of proof is a higher standard. It requires that you must be persuaded that it is highly probable that what the party seeks to prove is true.

You may have heard of a burden of proof used in criminal cases called "beyond a reasonable doubt." That burden of proof is the highest standard. It does not apply to a patent case such as this one, and you should therefore put it out of your mind.

I will now give you some background about the nature of this case and the issues you will be deciding. For each issue, I will instruct you as to the burden of proof that will apply. At the end of the trial I will review for you which burden of proof, either the more probable than not standard or the highly probable standard, to apply to each issue in this case.

Chapter Two
Patent Instructions

2.   Patent Instructions

2.1   The Parties and the Nature of the Case

As I have told you, this is a patent case. It involves U.S. Patent No. ___. Patents are often referred to by their last three digits. The patent in this case will be referred to as the _____ patent.

The _____ patent relates to [briefly describe technology involved]. During the trial the parties will offer testimony to familiarize you with this technology.

[Plaintiff], the plaintiff in this case, contends that [defendant], the defendant in this case, is infringing the _____ patent by its [making/using/selling/offering for sale/importing] _____. [Plaintiff] contends that it is entitled to damages caused by that infringement.

[Defendant] [denies that it is infringing and] contends that the _____ patent is [invalid and/or unenforceable] for a number of reasons that I will tell you about shortly.

First I will explain the U.S. patent system, the parts of a patent, and how a person obtains a patent.

2.2   The Patent System, Generally

Patents are issued by the United States Patent and Trademark Office, which is part of our government. The government is authorized by the United States Constitution to enact patent laws and issue patents to protect inventions. Inventions that are protected by patents may be of products, compositions, or of methods for doing something, or for using or making a product or composition.

The owner of a patent has the right, for the life of the patent, to prevent others from making, using, offering for sale, selling or importing the invention covered by the patent.

A patent is granted for a set period of time, which, in this case, is [20 years from the time the application for the _____ patent was filed/17 years from the date the _____ patent issued]. Once a patent expires, anyone is free to use the invention covered by the patent.

During the term of the patent, however, if another person makes, uses, offers to sell, sells or imports something that is covered by the patent without the patent owner's consent, that person is said to infringe the patent. The patent owner enforces a patent against persons believed to be infringers in a lawsuit in federal court, such as in this case.

To be entitled to patent protection an invention must be new, useful and nonobvious. A patent cannot legally take away the right to use that which was already known before the invention was made, or that which was obvious from what was already known. Thus, a patent will not be valid if it deprives people of the right to use old or known [products or processes], or of their right to use [products or processes] that were obvious at the time the invention was made. That which was already known at the time of the invention is called the "prior art." You will hear about the prior art relating to the _____ patent during the trial, and I will give you more instructions about what constitutes prior art at the end of the case.

2.3 The Parts of a Patent

A patent includes two basic parts: first, a written description of the invention, which may include drawings and which is referred to as the "specification" of the patent; and, second, the patent claims.

You have been provided with a copy of the _____ patent. Please refer to the patent as I identify its different sections.

The cover page of the _____ patent provides identifying information, including the date the patent issued and the patent number along the top, as well as the inventor's name, the filing date, [the assignee], and a list of the prior art publications considered in the Patent Office in issuing the patent.

The specification of the _____ patent begins with an abstract, found on the cover page. The abstract is a brief statement about the subject matter of the invention.

[Next are the drawings, which appear as Figures _____ to _____ on the next _____ pages. The drawings depict various aspects or features of the invention. They are described in words later in the patent specification.] The written description of the invention appears next. In this portion of the patent, each page is divided into two columns, which are numbered at the top of the page. The lines on each page are also numbered. The written description of the _____ patent begins at column 1, line 1, and continues to column _____, line _____. [It includes a background section, a summary of the invention, and a detailed description of the invention, including some specific examples.]

The specification is followed by one or more numbered paragraphs. These are called the claims. The claims may be divided into a number of [parts or steps], referred to as "claim limitations." In the _____ patent, the claims begin at column _____, line _____ and continue to the end of the patent, at column _____, line _____.

2.4   The Significance of Patent Claims

The claims of a patent are a main focus of a patent case because the claims define the patent owner's rights under the law. That is, the claims define what the patent owner may exclude others from doing during the term of the patent.

The claims of a patent serve two purposes. First, they state the boundaries of the invention. Second, they provide notice to the public of those boundaries. Thus, when a [product or process] is accused of infringing a patent, it is the patent claims that must be compared to the accused [product or process] to determine whether or not there is infringement. It is the claims of the patent that are infringed when patent infringement occurs. The claims are also at issue when the validity of a patent is challenged. In reaching your determinations with respect to infringement and invalidity, you must consider each claim separately.

In this case, we will be concerned with claims _____ of the _____ patent. [Plaintiff] contends that claims _____ are infringed. [Defendant] contends that claims _____ are [not infringed, and that they are invalid and unenforceable].

The language of patent claims may not be clear to you, or the parties may dispute its meaning. I will instruct you [now/at the end of the case] about the meaning of some of the claim language. You must use the meanings I give you when you decide the issues of infringement and invalidity.

NOTE

The claim constructions may be included in the preliminary instructions, or may be presented to the jury by counsel in their opening statements. If the constructions are included in the preliminary instructions, Instructions 6.1–6.6 should be included, as applicable, as well.

2.5   How a Patent Is Obtained

The U.S. Patent and Trademark Office is the agency of our government that examines patent applications and issues patents. When an applicant for a patent files an application with the Patent and Trademark Office, the application is assigned to a Patent Examiner. The Patent Examiner examines the application to determine whether or not the described invention meets the requirements for patentable inventions.

The Patent Examiner advises the applicant of his or her findings in a paper called an "office action." The Examiner may "reject" the claims if he or she believes they do not meet the requirements for patentable inventions. The applicant may respond to the rejection with arguments to support the claims, by making changes or amendments to the claims, or by submitting new claims. If the Examiner concludes that the legal requirements have all been satisfied, he or she "allows" the claims and a patent is issued.

This process, from the filing of the patent application to the issuance of the patent, is called "patent prosecution." The record of papers relating to the patent prosecution is referred to as the prosecution history or file history. The prosecution history becomes available to the public when the patent issues.

Chapter Three
Issues to Be Decided

3. Issues to Be Decided

I will now give you some information about the issues that will be presented to you at this trial and the law that you must follow in reaching your verdict. At the close of the trial, you will be given a verdict form and questions that you must answer in reaching your verdict. I will then give you more specific instructions to follow.

3.1 [Plaintiff's] Contentions

I will first describe [plaintiff's] contentions to you.

3.1.1 Direct Infringement

As I told you, [plaintiff] contends that [defendant] infringes claims _____ of the _____ patent by its [use, sale, offer for sale or import of product/use of process]. This is called direct infringement. [Plaintiff] seeks to prove direct infringement in one of two ways. The first is called "literal" infringement. To prove literal infringement, [plaintiff] must prove that it is more probable than not that [defendant's] [product or process] contains each and every limitation of one or more of the _____ patent claims.

The second way to prove direct infringement is by the "doctrine of equivalents." To prove infringement under the doctrine of equivalents, [plaintiff] must prove that it is more probable than not that, for each claim limitation not literally found in [defendant's] [product or process], the [product or process] contains an equivalent [structure or step]. In order to be equivalent, the differences between [plaintiff's] claim limitation and [defendant's] allegedly equivalent [structure or step] must be insubstantial. I will explain this in more detail in my final instructions.

[Identify the specific product/process accused of infringement and which claims are alleged to be infringed.]

3.1.2   Indirect Infringement

[Plaintiff] contends that [defendant] indirectly infringes claims _____ of the _____ patent by contributing to or encouraging others to directly infringe. There are two types of indirect infringement: contributory infringement and inducing infringement.

To prove contributory infringement of the _____ patent claims, [plaintiff] must prove that it is more probable than not that [defendant] sold or supplied to another person a component or part that is a material part of the patented invention and is not suitable for other uses. [Plaintiff] must also prove that the other person infringed the _____ patent claims, and that [defendant] knew that the component or part was especially made for use in an infringing manner.

To prove that [defendant] induced someone else to infringe the _____ patent claims, [plaintiff] must prove that it is more probable than not that [defendant] encouraged or instructed another person to [use a product or perform a process] in a manner that infringes, and that [defendant] knew or should have known that the encouragement or instructions would likely result in the other person infringing the claims.

3.1.3   Damages

[Plaintiff] claims that it has suffered damages as a result of [defendant's] infringement in the form of [lost profits that [plaintiff] would have made if [defendant] had not infringed [and/or] a reasonable royalty on each of [defendant's] sales of an infringing [product or process]]. I will explain to you at the end of the case [how lost profits are calculated [and/or] how a reasonable royalty is determined]. [Plaintiff] must prove the damages it has suffered as a result of [defendant's] infringement by the more probable than not standard.

3.1.4   Willful Infringement

[Plaintiff] asserts that [defendant] has knowingly and willfully infringed the _____ patent claims. To prove willful infringement, [plaintiff] must prove that [defendant] knew of the _____ patent, and that [defendant] did not have a reasonable belief either that the patent was invalid [or unenforceable] or that it did not infringe the patent.

Asserting willful infringement requires a higher burden of proof—the highly probable standard—than [plaintiff's] other claims, which require proof by the more probable than not standard. I will explain in more detail at the end of the case how you decide whether [defendant] willfully infringed [plaintiff's] patent claims or not.

3.2 [Defendant's] Contentions

I will now instruct you on [defendant's] contentions.

3.2.1 Invalidity

[Defendant] contends that claims _____ of the _____ patent are invalid for a number of reasons. Although the Patent and Trademark Office issued the _____ patent, it is your job to determine whether or not the legal requirements of patentability were met; that is, it is your job to determine whether or not the _____ patent is invalid.

I will now briefly explain to you the legal requirements for each of the grounds of [defendant's] contention that the _____ patent claims are invalid. I will provide more details for each ground in my final instructions.

3.2.2　　　Anticipation

[Defendant] contends that the invention recited in claims
_____ of the _____ patent is not new. An invention that
is not new is said to be "anticipated" by the prior art. In order
to prove that a claim is anticipated by the prior art, [defen-
dant] must prove that it is highly probable that each and
every limitation of the claim is present in a single item of prior
art.

3.2.3   Obviousness

[Defendant] contends that the invention recited in claims _____ of the _____ patent are invalid for obviousness. A patent claim will be invalid, even if it is not anticipated by the prior art, if the invention recited in the claim would have been obvious to a person of ordinary skill in the field of the invention at the time it was made. The ordinary skilled person is a person of average education and training in the field of the invention and is presumed to be aware of all of the relevant prior art. You will hear evidence about the skill and experience of such a person during the course of the trial.

In order to prove invalidity based on obviousness, [defendant] must prove that it is highly probable that the invention recited in the patent claims would have been obvious to a person of ordinary skill in the field of invention at the time the invention was made. I will instruct you at the end of the case how to determine when the invention was made.

3.2.4   Written Description/Claiming Requirements

[Defendant] contends that claims _____ of the _____ patent are invalid because the patent does not contain [a written description/an enabling description/a description of the best mode of the invention/definite claims].

[Use only those of the following paragraphs that apply]:

1. The description in the patent specification of the invention must be complete. This is referred to as the "written description requirement." In order to prove that claims _____ of the _____ patent are invalid for lack of a written description, [defendant] must prove that it is highly probable that the specification does not contain a description of each and every limitation of those patent claims.

2. The patent specification must contain enough detail to enable a skilled person reading the patent to make and use the invention. This is referred to as the "enablement requirement." In order to prove that claims _____ of the _____ patent are invalid for lack of an enabling description, [defendant] must prove that it is highly probable that the specification does not contain enough information to teach a skilled person how to make and use the claimed invention without undue experimentation.

3. The patent specification must describe the best way, or mode, of making and using the invention known to the inventor at the time the application was filed. This is referred to as the "best mode requirement." In order to prove that claims _____ of the _____ patent are invalid for failure to disclose the best mode of the invention, [defendant] must prove that it is highly probable that, first, at the time the application was filed, the inventor knew of a best mode of making and using the claimed invention, and, second, that the _____ patent does not describe that best mode.

4. [Defendant] contends that claims _____ of the _____ patent are invalid because they are "indefinite." The claims must be definite enough so that a skilled person reading them knows what is covered by the claims and what is

not. [Defendant] must prove that the claims are indefinite by the highly probable standard.

I will explain in more detail at the end of the case how you decide the issue[s] of [written description/enablement/best mode/definiteness].

3.2.5 Inequitable Conduct

[Defendant] contends that [plaintiff] may not enforce the _____ patent because [plaintiff] engaged in inequitable conduct before the Patent and Trademark Office when it obtained the _____ patent. To prove that inequitable conduct occurred, [defendant] must prove that it is highly probable that the patent applicant, or the applicant's attorney or representative, withheld or misrepresented material information, and did so with an intent to mislead or deceive the Patent and Trademark Office.

I will provide you with more details about inequitable conduct at the end of the case.

Part II–Final Instructions

Chapter Four
The Parties and Their Contentions

4. The Parties and Their Contentions

I will now review for you the parties in this action and the positions of the parties that you will have to consider in reaching your verdict.

4.1 The Parties and the Nature of the Case

As I have told you, this is a patent case. It involves U.S. Patent No. _____. Patents are often referred to by their last three digits. The patent in this case will be referred to as the _____ patent.

The _____ patent relates to [briefly describe technology involved]. During the trial the parties will offer testimony to familiarize you with this technology.

4.2 [Plaintiff's] Contentions

[Plaintiff], the plaintiff in this case, contends that [defendant], the defendant in this case, is infringing the _____ patent by its [making/using/selling/offering for sale/importing] _____. [Plaintiff] contends that it is entitled to damages caused by that infringement.

4.3   [Defendant's] Contentions

[Defendant] [denies that it is infringing and] contends that the _____ patent is [invalid and/or unenforceable] for a number of reasons that I will tell you about shortly.

4.4   Summary of Patent Issues and Burdens of Proof

This section should set forth the issues that are involved in a particular case.

Chapter Five
The Patent System

5.   The Patent System

At the beginning of the trial, I gave you some general information about patents and the patent system, and a brief overview of the patent laws relevant to this case. I will now give you more detailed instructions about the patent laws that specifically relate to this case. If you would like to review my instructions at any time during your deliberations, they will be available to you in the jury room.

Chapter Six
The Claims of the Patent in Suit

6.   The Claims of the Patent in Suit

As I told you at the beginning of the trial, the claims of a patent are the numbered sentences at the end of the patent. The claims describe the invention made by the inventor and describe what the patent owner owns and, therefore, controls what the patent owner may prevent others from doing. Claims may describe products, such as machines or chemical compounds, or processes for making or using a product.

Claims are usually divided into parts or steps, called "limitations." For example, a claim that covers the invention of a table may recite the tabletop, four legs and the glue that secures the legs to the tabletop. The tabletop, legs and glue are each a separate limitation of the claim.

6.1   Construction of the Claims

In deciding whether or not an accused [process or product] infringes a patent, the first step is to understand the meaning of the words used in the patent claims.

It is my job as Judge to determine what the patent claims mean and to instruct you about that meaning. You must accept the meanings I give you and use them when you decide whether or not the patent is infringed, and whether or not it is invalid [and unenforceable].

[If claim constructions are being provided to the jury for the first time in the final instructions:]

Before I instruct you about the meaning of the words of the claims, I will explain to you the different types of claims that are at issue in this case.

[If claim constructions were provided in the preliminary instructions:]

At the start of the trial, I instructed you about the meaning of the words of the claims and the different types of claims that are at issue in this case. I will now review those instructions with you again.

It may be helpful to refer to the copy of the _____ patent that you have been given as I discuss the claims at issue here. The claims are at the end of the patent, starting in column _____. [I will be giving you a list of the claims at issue as part of the verdict form when I conclude my instructions.]

NOTE

In *Markman* v. *Westview Instruments, Inc.*, 517 U.S. 370 (1996), the United States Supreme Court upheld the Federal Circuit holding that claim construction is a matter of law exclusively for the court. Thus, the district court is to instruct the jury as to how the claim language should be construed. The jury will then use this construction in its deliberations on both the infringement and validity issues.

The Supreme Court and subsequent Federal Circuit decisions have in large measure left to the district court's discretion the procedural mechanism for construing the patent claims and the timing of instructing the jury on the construction. The court may instruct the jury as to its claim construction during its preliminary instructions, final instructions, or both. Alternatively, counsel may present the court's construction in their opening statements.

The types of evidence that may be used in construing patent claims, and the weight to be accorded that evidence, have been the subject of numerous Federal Circuit decisions. In the *Markman* Federal Circuit decision, the *en banc* court identified two types of evidence to be used in claim construction: "intrinsic evidence," which includes the patent specification, the language of other claims, the patent's prosecution history, and the prior art cited during prosecution; and "extrinsic evidence," which includes expert opinions, dictionary definitions, inventor testimony, and prior art not cited during prosecution. 52 F.3d 967, 977 (Fed. Cir. 1995) (*en banc*).

In *Vitronics Corp. v. Conceptronic, Inc.*, 90 F.3d 1576, 1582 (Fed. Cir. 1996), the Federal Circuit emphasized that intrinsic evidence should be the primary type of evidence used in claim construction. In subsequent decisions, the Federal Circuit has made it clear, however, that "[a]ll intrinsic evidence is not equal." *Interactive Gift Express, Inc. v. CompuServe, Inc.*, 256 F.3d 1323, 1331 (Fed. Cir. 2001). "In construing claims, the analytical focus must begin and remain centered on the language of the claims themselves, for it is that language that the patentee chose to use to 'particularly point[ ] out and distinctly claim[ ] the subject matter which the patentee regards as his invention.'" *Id.* (citation omitted).

In general, the words of a claim are to be given their ordinary and accustomed meaning to one of skill in the art. *Johnson Worldwide Assocs., Inc. v. Zebco Corp.*, 175 F.3d 985, 988–90 (Fed. Cir. 1999). Exceptions occur where the patent explicitly defines a claim term and adoption of the ordinary and accustomed meaning would render the claim indefinite. *Id.*

The Federal Circuit also has identified a third situation in which it may be appropriate to adopt a claim construction that varies from the claim language's ordinary and accustomed meaning. The Court held that "[w]here the specification makes clear that the invention does not include a particular feature, that feature is deemed to be outside the reach of the claims of the patent, even though the language of the claims, read without reference to the specification, might be considered broad enough to encompass the feature in question." *SciMed Life Systems, Inc.* v. *Advanced Cardiovascular Sys.*, 242 F.3d 1337, 1341 (Fed. Cir. 2001).

The role of extrinsic evidence in claim construction has been the subject of substantial discussion in the case law. Notwithstanding the Federal Circuit's clear statement in *Markman* that extrinsic evidence may be used in appropriate circumstances, some courts have interpreted the Federal Circuit's decision in *Vitronics* to preclude the use of extrinsic evidence in claim construction. *See Minuteman Int'l, Inc.* v. *Critical-Vac Filtration Corp.*, No. 95C 7255, 1997 WL 187326, at *2 (N.D. Ill. April 11, 1997) ("the admission of extrinsic evidence is improper unless there remains 'some genuine ambiguity in the claims, after consideration of all available intrinsic evidence'") (citation omitted); *Rival Co.* v. *Sunbeam Corp.*, 987 F. Supp. 1167, 1171 (W.D. Miss. 1997) ("The theory behind the admission of intrinsic evidence, and the exclusion of extrinsic evidence, has been explained by the Federal Circuit . . . [in *Vitronics*]"), *aff'd without op.*, 185 F.3d 885 (Fed. Cir. 1999).

Federal Circuit decisions subsequent to *Vitronics* have reiterated that extrinsic evidence may be considered in claim construction, as long as it is not used to vary or contradict the intrinsic evidence. *See Pitney Bowes, Inc.* v. *Hewlett-Packard Co.*, 182 F.3d 1298, 1308 (Fed. Cir. 1999) ("Despite the district court's statements to the contrary, *Vitronics* does not prohibit courts from examining extrinsic evidence, even when the patent document is clear."); *AFG Indus., Inc.* v. *Cardinal IG Co.*, 239 F.3d 1239, 1249 (Fed. Cir. 2001) (failure to consider testimony of persons of ordinary skill when construing claims may be reversible error).

AUTHORITIES

Markman v. *Westview Instruments, Inc.*, 517 U.S. 370, 384–391 (1996); *Bell Atlantic Network Servs., Inc.* v. *Covad Communications Group, Inc.*, 262 F.3d 1258, 1267 (Fed. Cir. 2001); *Interactive Gift Express, Inc.* v. *CompuServe, Inc.*, 256 F.3d 1323, 1331 (Fed. Cir. 2001); *SciMed Life Systems, Inc.* v. *Advanced Cardiovascular Sys.*, 242 F.3d 1337, 1341 (Fed. Cir. 2001); *AFG Indus., Inc.* v. *Cardinal IG Co.*, 239 F.3d 1239, 1244–45 (Fed. Cir. 2001); *Hill-Rom Co.* v. *Kinetic Concepts, Inc.*, 209 F.3d 1337, 1340–41 (Fed. Cir. 2000); *Pitney Bowes, Inc.* v. *Hewlett-Packard Co.*, 182 F.3d 1298, 1304–06 (Fed. Cir. 1999); *Johnson Worldwide Assocs., Inc.* v. *Zebco Corp.*, 175 F.3d 985, 988–90 (Fed. Cir. 1999); *Cybor Corp.* v. *FAS Techs., Inc.*, 138 F.3d 1448, 1455–56 (Fed. Cir. 1998); *Vitronics Corp.* v. *Conceptronic, Inc.*, 90 F.3d 1576, 1581–84 (Fed. Cir. 1996); *Markman* v. *Westview Instruments, Inc.*, 52 F.3d 967, 977 (Fed. Cir. 1995) (*en banc*); *Rival Co.* v. *Sunbeam Corp.*, 987 F. Supp. 1167, 1171 (W.D. Miss. 1997) *aff'd without op.*, 185 F.3d 885 (Fed. Cir. 1999); *Minuteman Int'l, Inc.* v. *Critical-Vac Filtration Corp.*, No. 95C 7255, 1997 WL 187326, at *2 (N.D. Ill. April 11, 1997).

6.2   Independent and Dependent Claims

Patent claims may exist in two forms, referred to as independent claims and dependent claims. An independent claim does not refer to any other claim of the patent. Thus it is not necessary to look at any other claim to determine what an independent claim covers. Claim _____ of the _____ patent, for example, is an independent claim.

A dependent claim refers to at least one other claim in the patent. A dependent claim includes each of the limitations of the other claim or claims to which it refers, as well as the additional limitations recited in the dependent claim itself. Therefore, to determine what a dependent claim covers, it is necessary to look at both the dependent claim and the other claim or claims to which it refers.

For example, claim _____ is a dependent claim. It refers to claim _____. To determine what dependent claim _____ covers, the words of that claim and the words of claim _____ must be read together.

NOTE

If numerous dependent claims or complicated multiple dependencies exist, consider providing the jurors with a table setting out the relationships of the asserted claims to each other.

AUTHORITIES

35 U.S.C. § 112 ¶ 4 (1984); *Globetrotter Software, Inc.* v. *Elan Computer Group, Inc.*, 236 F.3d 1363, 1369–70 (Fed. Cir. 2001); *Dow Chem. Co.* v. *United States*, 226 F.3d 1334, 1341–42 (Fed. Cir. 2000); *Sibia Neurosciences, Inc.* v. *Cadus Pharm. Corp.*, 225 F.3d 1349, 1359 (Fed. Cir. 2000); *Wolverine World Wide, Inc.* v. *Nike, Inc.*, 38 F.3d 1192, 1199 (Fed. Cir. 1994); *Carroll Touch, Inc.* v. *Electro Mech. Sys., Inc.*, 15 F.3d 1573, 1576 (Fed. Cir. 1993); *Marsh-McBirney, Inc.* v. *Montedoro-Whitney Corp.*, 882 F.2d 498, 504 (Fed. Cir. 1989); *Wahpeton Canvas Co., Inc.* v. *Frontier, Inc.*, 870 F.2d 1546, 1552–23 (Fed. Cir. 1989).

6.3   Product-by-Process Claims

Sometimes a product may best be described by the process by which it is made, instead of by describing its structure or chemical characteristics. Such claims are called "product-by-process" claims.

Claims _____ of the _____ patent are product-by-process claims.

NOTE

This instruction may be included in the claim construction or read separately.

AUTHORITIES

Vanguard Prods. Corp. v. Parker Hannifin Corp., 234 F.3d 1370, 1372–73 (Fed. Cir. 2000); *Exxon Chem. Patents, Inc. v. Lubrizol Corp.*, 64 F.3d 1553, 1557–58 (Fed. Cir. 1995); *Mentor Corp. v. Colopast, Inc.*, 998 F.2d 992, 997 (Fed. Cir. 1993); *Atl. Thermoplastics Co. v. Faytex Corp.*, 970 F.2d 834, 837 (Fed. Cir. 1992), *reh'g en banc denied*, 974 F.2d 1279 (Fed. Cir. 1992); *Scripps Clinic & Research Found. v. Genentech, Inc.*, 927 F.2d 1565, 1583 (Fed. Cir. 1991).

6.4   Means-plus-Function Claim Limitations

Some patent claim limitations may describe a "means" for performing a function, rather than describing the structure that performs the function. For example, let's assume a patent describes a table where the legs are glued to the tabletop. One way to claim the table is to recite the tabletop, four legs and glue between the legs and the tabletop. Another way to claim the table is to recite the tabletop and the legs, but, rather than recite the glue, recite a "means for securing the legs to the tabletop." This second type of claim limitation is called a "means-plus-function" limitation. It describes a means for performing the function of securing the legs to the tabletop, rather than expressly reciting the glue.

When a claim limitation is in means-plus-function form, it covers the structures described in the patent specification for performing the function stated in the claim, as well as any structure that is equivalent to the described structures. In our example, the claim covers a table using glue to secure the legs to the tabletop, as described in the patent, and any equivalent structure that performs the function of securing the legs to the tabletop.

Claims _____ of the _____ patent include means-plus-function limitations. In instructing you about the meaning of a means-plus-function claim limitation, I will tell you, first, the function that each of the means-plus-function claim limitations performs, and, second, the structure disclosed in the patent specification that corresponds to each means-plus-function limitation.

NOTE

35 U.S.C. § 112, ¶ 6 (1984) states that:

> An element in a claim for a combination may be expressed as a means or step for performing a specified function without the recital of structure, material, or acts in support thereof, and such claim shall be construed to cover the corresponding structure, material, or acts described in the specification and equivalents thereof.

Thus, a patent owner may claim an invention in functional, rather than structural, terms. If a patent owner drafts the claims pursuant to § 112, ¶ 6, the patent owner must describe in the patent specification a structure that corresponds to the claimed function. In interpreting § 112, ¶ 6 limitations, it is the court's responsibility as part of claim construction to identify the structure, if any, that corresponds to the claimed function and to instruct the jury accordingly.

This instruction may be included in the claim construction, or it can be read separately if the Court concludes as a matter of law that the claims contain one or more means-plus-function limitations. It may be useful to provide the jury with copies of the patent in which the patent specification is keyed to the specific means-plus-function claim limitations.

AUTHORITIES

35 U.S.C. § 112 ¶ 6 (1984); *BBA Nonwovens Simpsonville, Inc.* v. *Superior Nonwovens, LLC*, 303 F.3d 1322 (Fed. Cir. 2002); *Masco Corp.* v. *United States*, 303 F.3d 1316 (Fed. Cir. 2002); *Allen Eng'g Corp.* v. *Bartell Indus.*, 299 F.3d 1336, 1347–48 (Fed. Cir. 2002); *IMS Tech., Inc.* v. *Haas Automation, Inc.*, 206 F.3d 1422, 1435–37 (Fed. Cir. 2000); *Odetics, Inc.* v. *Storage Tech. Corp.*, 185 F.3d 1259, 1266–68 (Fed. Cir. 1999); *WMS Gaming Inc.* v. *Int'l Game Tech.*, 184 F.3d 1339, 1347–50 (Fed. Cir. 1999); *Al-Site Corp.* v. *VSI Int'l, Inc.*, 174 F.3d 1308, 1318–21 (Fed. Cir. 1999); *Chiuminatta Concrete Concepts, Inc.* v. *Cardinal Indus., Inc.*, 145 F.3d 1303, 1307–10 (Fed. Cir. 1998); *B. Braun Med. Inc.* v. *Abbott Labs.*, 124 F.3d 1419, 1424–25 (Fed. Cir. 1997).

6.5 Transitional Phrases—Introduction

Most claims contain a transitional phrase between the opening clause of the claim, known as the preamble, and the body of the claim. The most common transitional phrases are "comprising," "consisting of," and "consisting essentially of." Each of these phrases has a special meaning in patent law, which impacts the literal scope of the claim.

"Comprising" is the most open-ended of the three transitional phrases. When "comprising" is used, a claim includes products or processes containing the limitations recited in the claim plus additional elements or steps. Other transitional phrases, such as "including" and "having," have also been construed to include products or processes containing elements or steps in addition to those recited in the claim. *See, e.g., Crystal Semiconductor Corp. v. Tritech Microelecs. Int'l, Inc.,* 246 F.3d 1336, 1348 (Fed. Cir. 2001) ("The transition 'having' can also make a claim open."); *Hewlett-Packard Co. v. Repeat-O-Type Stencil Mfg. Corp.,* 123 F.3d 1445, 1451 (Fed. Cir. 1997) ("The claim term 'including' is synonymous with 'comprising,' thereby permitting the inclusion of unnamed components.").

The transitional phrase "consisting of" is the most limited of the three phrases. A patent claim with the transitional phrase "consisting of" includes products or processes that only contain the specific limitations recited in the claim. It does not, however, preclude a finding of infringement by products or processes containing additional elements or steps under the doctrine of equivalents. *See Vehicular Techs. Corp. v. Titan Wheel Int'l., Inc.,* 141 F.3d 1084, 1092 (Fed. Cir. 1998).

The transitional phrase "consisting essentially of" also limits the scope of a claimed invention, but not as severely as "consisting of." Claims using "consisting essentially of" exclude products or processes containing additional elements or steps that "materially affect the basic and novel characteristics" of the claimed invention. *See AFG Indus., Inc. v. Cardinal IG Co.,* 239 F.3d 1239, 1245 (Fed. Cir. 2001). In *AFG,* the Federal Circuit interpreted the transitional phrase "composed of" to impart to the claim the same scope as "consisting essentially of." *Id.* The Court pointed to the patent specification and other evidence to determine that the term "composed of" is "not completely closed" and, therefore, the claims should have the same scope as claims with the "consisting essentially of" transitional phrase.

6.5.1 "Comprising" Claims

The beginning portion, or preamble, of claims _____ of the
_____ patent uses the word "comprising." "Comprising"
means "including" or "containing." A claim that uses the
word "comprising" or "comprises" is not limited to [products
or processes] having only the [elements or steps] that are recited in the claim, but also covers [products or processes] that
add additional [elements or steps].

Let's take our example of the claim that covers a table. If the
claim recites a table "comprising" a tabletop, legs and glue,
the claim will cover any table that contains these structures,
even if the table also contains other structures, such as a leaf
or wheels on the legs.

NOTE

This instruction may be included in the claim construction or
read separately.

AUTHORITIES

Vehicular Techs. Corp. v. *Titan Wheel Int'l, Inc.,* 212 F.3d 1377,
1382–83 (Fed. Cir. 2000); *Vivid Techs., Inc.* v. *Am. Sci. & Eng'g,
Inc.,* 200 F.3d 795, 811–12 (Fed. Cir. 1999); *Georgia-Pacific Corp.*
v. *United States Gypsum Co.,* 195 F.3d 1322, 1327–29 (Fed. Cir.
1999); *Elkay Mfg. Co.* v. *Ebco Mfg. Co.,* 192 F.3d 973, 977 (Fed.
Cir. 1999); *Spectrum Int'l, Inc.* v. *Sterilite Corp.,* 164 F.3d 1372,
1379–80 (Fed. Cir. 1998); *Phillips Petroleum Co.* v. *Huntsman
Polymers Corp.,* 157 F.3d 866, 874 (Fed. Cir. 1998); *Stiftung* v.
Renishaw PLC, 945 F.2d 1173, 1177–79 (Fed. Cir. 1991).

6.5.2   "Consisting Essentially Of" Claims

The beginning portion, or preamble, of claims _____ of the _____ patent uses the language "consisting essentially of." If a patent claim uses the words "consisting essentially of," then a [product or process] containing additional [structures or steps] beyond those recited in the claim may be covered by the claim, but only if those additional [structures or steps] do not materially affect the basic and novel characteristics of the claimed invention.

Looking again at our table example, if the claim recited a table "consisting essentially of" a tabletop, legs and glue, the claim would cover the table with wheels on the legs only if the wheels did not change the basic and novel characteristics of the table.

NOTE

This instruction may be included in the claim construction or read separately.

AUTHORITIES

AFG Indus., Inc. v. *Cardinal IG Co.*, 239 F.3d 1239, 1245 (Fed. Cir. 2001); *PPG Indus.* v. *Guardian Indus. Corp.*, 156 F.3d 1351, 1354–55 (Fed. Cir. 1998); *Atlas Powder Co.* v. *E.I. DuPont de Nemours & Co.*, 750 F.2d 1569, 1573–74 (Fed. Cir. 1984).

6.5.3   "Consisting Of" Claims

Claims _____ of the _____ patent use the words "consisting of." The words "consisting of" in a patent claim limit the [structures or steps] covered by the claim. A patent claim that uses "consisting of" is limited to only those [limitations or steps] that follow it in the claim. Thus, a "consisting of" claim will not cover a [product or process] that contains [structures or steps] beyond those recited in the claim.

Looking again at our table example, if the claim recites a table "consisting of" a tabletop, legs and glue, the claim will only cover tables that contain these three limitations, and nothing more. In other words, the addition of an extra structure, such as wheels on the legs, is not covered by the claim.

NOTE

This instruction may be included in the claim construction or read separately.

AUTHORITIES

Vehicular Techs. Corp. v. *Titan Wheel Int'l*, 212 F.3d 1377, 1382–83 (Fed. Cir. 2000); *Georgia-Pacific Corp.* v. *United States Gypsum Co.*, 195 F.3d 1322, 1327–28 (Fed. Cir. 1999); *Mannesmann Demag Corp.* v. *Engineered Metal Prods. Co.*, 793 F.2d 1279, 1282 (Fed. Cir. 1986).

6.6   Limitations of the Claims at Issue

I have now instructed you as to the types of claims at issue in this case. I will next define the meaning of the words used in the patent claims at issue. You must use the definitions I provide to you in your consideration of the infringement and invalidity issues.

[Construction of the claims to be supplied by the Court.]

Chapter Seven
Infringement—Introduction

# 7.	Infringement—Introduction

35 U.S.C. § 271(a) (Supp. 2001) provides:

> Except as otherwise provided in this title, whoever, without authority makes, uses, offers to sell, or sells any patented invention, within the United States or imports into the United States any patented invention during the term of the patent therefor, infringes the patent.

This section sets forth the basis of a patent owner's right to exclude others from practicing the patented invention. It does not, however, grant to the patent owner the right to practice the patented invention. In practicing the patented invention, a patent owner may infringe another's patent.

The patent owner has the burden of proving infringement by a preponderance of the evidence. A direct infringement analysis entails two steps. First, the court must construe the claims to determine their proper scope. Second, the jury must determine whether or not the accused device falls within the scope of the properly construed claims. *Markman* v. *Westview Instruments, Inc.*, 52 F.3d 967, 976 (Fed. Cir. 1995) (*en banc*), *aff'd*, 517 U.S. 370 (1995). Infringement may be literal (i.e., the accused product or process literally includes each and every recited limitation) or under the doctrine of equivalents (i.e., for each claim limitation not literally present, the accused product or process includes an element or step that is not substantially different from the missing limitation).

In order to reach its verdict on infringement, the jury need not always be instructed on the doctrine of equivalents. If a patent owner only asserts literal infringement, the jury instruction may be so limited, and Instruction 7.2 should be used. If a patent owner only asserts infringement under the doctrine of equivalents, or asserts alternatively literal infringement and infringement under the doctrine of equivalents, then the jury should be instructed on both types of infringement and Instruction 7.3 should be used.

7.1   Patent Infringement, Generally—Direct Infringement

A patent owner has the right to stop others from using the invention covered by its patent claims during the life of the patent. If any person makes, uses, sells or offers to sell [or imports] what is covered by the patent claims without the patent owner's permission, that person is said to infringe the patent. This type of infringement is called "direct infringement." [In addition to enforcing a patent against a direct infringer, a patent owner also has the right to enforce the patent against those who are known as "indirect infringers."]

Only the claims of a patent can be infringed. You must compare patent claims _____, as I have defined them, to the accused [product or process], and determine whether or not there is infringement. You should not compare [defendant's] [product or process] with any specific example set out in the patent, or with [plaintiff's] product or process. The only correct comparison is with the language of the claim itself, with the meaning I have given you.

You must consider each claim individually and must reach your decision as to each assertion of infringement based on my instructions about the meaning and scope of the claims, the legal requirements for infringement, and the evidence presented to you by the parties. I will first discuss direct infringement.

Whether or not [defendant] knew that what it was doing was an infringement does not matter. A person may be found to be a direct infringer of a patent even if he or she believed in good faith that what he or she was doing was not an infringement of any patent, and even if he or she did not even know of the patent.

In this case, [plaintiff] asserts that [defendant's] [product or process] directly infringes claims _____ of the _____ patent. It is your job to determine whether or not [plaintiff] has proved by the more probable than not standard that defendant has directly infringed any of claims _____ of the _____ patent.

AUTHORITIES

35 U.S.C. §§ 271–281 (1984 & Supp. 2001); *Warner-Jenkinson Co. v. Hilton Davis Chemical Co.*, 520 U.S. 17, 36 (1997); *Fla. Prepaid Postsecondary Educ. Expense Bd. v. College Sav. Bank*, 527 U.S. 627, 644 (1999); *DeMarini Sports, Inc. v. Worth, Inc.*, 239 F.3d 1314, 1330 (Fed. Cir. 2001); *Payless Shoesource, Inc. v. Reebok Int'l Ltd.*, 998 F.2d 985, 990 (Fed. Cir. 1993); *Atl. Thermoplastics Co. v. Faytex Corp.*, 974 F.2d 1299, 1300 (Fed. Cir. 1992); *Intel Corp. v. United States Int'l Trade Comm'n*, 946 F.2d 821, 832 (Fed. Cir. 1991); *Loctite Corp. v. Ultraseal Ltd.*, 781 F.2d 861, 867 (Fed. Cir. 1985).

7.2   Literal Infringement

In order to infringe a patent claim, a [product or process] must include every limitation of the claim. If [defendant's] [product or process] omits even a single [structure or step] recited in a claim, then you must find that [defendant] has not infringed that claim. You must consider each of the patent claims separately.

A claim limitation is present in an accused [product or process] if it exists in the [product or process] just as it is described in the claim language, either as I have explained that language to you or, if I did not explain it, as you understand it.

NOTE

This instruction should be used when infringement under the doctrine of equivalents is not an issue in the case.

AUTHORITIES

Rosco, Inc. v. *Mirror Lite Co.*, 304 F.3d 1373 (Fed. Cir. 2002); *Tate Access Floors, Inc.* v. *Interface Architectural Res.*, 279 F.3d 1357, 1366 (Fed. Cir. 2002); *Smith & Nephew, Inc.* v. *Ethicon, Inc.*, 276 F.3d 1304, 1311 (Fed. Cir. 2001).

7.3 Infringement—Every Claim Limitation Must Be Present, Either Literally or under the Doctrine of Equivalents

In order to infringe a patent claim, a [product or process] must include every limitation of the claim. If [defendant's] [product or process] omits even a single [structure or step] recited in a claim, then you must find that [defendant] has not infringed that claim. You must consider each of the patent claims separately.

A claim limitation may be present in an accused [product or process] in one of two ways: either literally or under what is known as the doctrine of equivalents. A claim limitation is literally present if it exists in the accused [product or process] just as it is described in the claim language, either as I have explained that language to you or, if I did not explain it, as you understand it.

A claim limitation is present in an accused [product or process] under the doctrine of equivalents if the differences between the claim limitation and a comparable element of the accused [product or process] are insubstantial. One way to determine this is to look at whether or not the accused [product or process] performs substantially the same function, in substantially the same way, to achieve substantially the same result as the claimed invention.

Another way to determine whether the differences are insubstantial is to consider whether or not people of ordinary skill in the field of the invention believe that the [structure or step] of the accused [product or process] and the [structure or step] recited in the patent claim limitation are interchangeable. A person of ordinary skill is a person with average education and training in the field. The belief of such a person must be based on what was known at the time of the activities which constitute the alleged infringement, and not what was known at the time the patent application was filed or when the patent issued. Thus, the inventor need not have foreseen, and the patent need not describe, all potential equivalents to the invention covered by the claims. Also, slight changes in technique or improvements made possible by technology developed after the patent application is filed may still be considered equivalent for the purposes of the doctrine of equivalents.

[The following paragraphs should be used in addition to the above paragraphs in cases involving chemical compounds or chemical compositions]:

As I have explained to you, claims _____ of the _____ patent are directed to a chemical compound or composition made up of certain listed ingredients. If you find that the accused product does not literally include every limitation of these claims because of changes to one or more of the ingredients, you may use another test to decide whether the changed ingredient is equivalent to the ingredient listed in the claim. That test is whether or not the changed ingredient has the same purpose, quality and function as the claimed ingredient. In other words, you must consider whether the new ingredient in the accused product and the ingredient listed in the claim serve the same purpose, have the same qualities when combined with the other ingredients of the chemical compound or composition, and perform the same function.

NOTE

This instruction should be used instead of Instruction 7.2 when infringement under the doctrine of equivalents is an issue in the case, either alone or with a claim of literal infringement.

In *Warner-Jenkinson Co.* v. *Hilton-Davis Chem. Co.*, 520 U.S. 17 (1997), the Supreme Court confirmed the viability of the doctrine of equivalents as a basis for an infringement finding. The Court also confirmed the standard to be used for determining whether or not an accused product or process contains an element or step that is equivalent to a claim limitation. An element or step is equivalent to a claim limitation if the differences between that element or step and the claim limitation are insubstantial. *Id.* at 40. The Supreme Court left it to the Federal Circuit to identify specific tests to be used in determining whether or not such differences are insubstantial. *Id.*

This instruction sets out the most commonly used "function-way-result" and "known interchangeability" tests for infringement under the doctrine of equivalents. *Id.* at 25; *see also Graver Tank & Mfg. Co. v. Linde Air Prods. Co.*, 339 U.S. 605, 609 (1950). It also sets out the "purpose, quality and function" test used with claims directed to chemical compositions. *Warner-Jenkinson*, 520 U.S. at 25; *see also Graver Tank*, 339 U.S. at 609. Left for the argument of counsel are the factors that have been identified in the case law for determining the range of equivalents to which the claim limitations are entitled.

For example, courts have held that "pioneering inventions," *i.e.*, inventions that represent major advances over the prior art, are entitled to a broad range of equivalents. The Federal Circuit has moved away from this label, stating in one case that an inventor's alleged status as a "pioneer" does not automatically entitle the inventor to claims with a broad range of equivalents. *See Augustine Med., Inc. v. Gaymar Indus., Inc.*, 181 F.3d 1291, 1301–02 (Fed. Cir. 1999): the Court explained that it is the claim scope, as defined by the claim language, and the absence of prior art (which results in the absence of amendments narrowing the claims in light of prior art) that entitle a patent claim to a broad range of equivalents.

Although at least one post-*Warner-Jenkinson* decision states that evidence of copying may be relevant to infringement under the doctrine of equivalents, *Advanced Display Sys., Inc. v. Kent State Univ.*, 212 F.3d 1272, 1287 (Fed. Cir. 2000), *Warner-Jenkinson* makes it clear that "intent plays no role in the application of the doctrine of equivalents." 520 U.S. 17, 36 (1997). *See also Allen Eng'g Corp. v. Bartell Indus., Inc.*, 299 F.3d 1633, 1351 (Fed. Cir. 2002); *DeMarini Sports, Inc. v. Worth, Inc.*, 239 F.3d 1314, 1334 (Fed. Cir. 2001); *Moore U.S.A., Inc. v. Standard Register Co.*, 229 F.3d 1091, 1107 (Fed. Cir. 2000).

AUTHORITIES

Warner-Jenkinson Co. v. Hilton Davis Chem. Co., 520 U.S. 17, 37 (1997); *Graver Tank & Mfg. Co. v. Linde Air Prods. Co.*, 339 U.S. 605, 609 (1950); *Allen Eng'g Corp. v. Bartell Indus., Inc.*, 299 F.3d 1336, 1351 (Fed. Cir. 2002); *Riles v. Shell Exploration and Prod. Co.*, 298 F.3d 1302, 1309–10 (Fed. Cir. 2002); *DeMarini Sports, Inc. v. Worth, Inc.*, 239 F.3d 1314, 1334 (Fed. Cir. 2001); *Biovail Corp. Int'l v. Andrx Pharms., Inc.*, 239 F.3d 1297, 1302–03 (Fed. Cir. 2001); *Moore U.S.A., Inc. v. Standard Register Co.*, 229 F.3d 1091, 1107 (Fed. Cir. 2000); *Advanced Display Sys., Inc. v. Kent State Univ.*, 212 F.3d 1272, 1287 (Fed. Cir. 2000); *Bayer AG v. Elan Pharm., Research Corp.*, 212 F.3d 1241, 1247–50 (Fed. Cir. 2000); *Augustine Med., Inc. v. Gaymar Indus., Inc.*, 181 F.3d 1291, 1301–02 (Fed. Cir. 1999); *Pennwalt Corp. v. Durand-Wayland, Inc.*, 833 F.2d 931, 934 (Fed. Cir. 1987) (*en banc*).

7.4   Limitations on the Doctrine of Equivalents

The patent law places certain limits on the doctrine of equivalents. It is my duty to decide whether or not any of these limits apply in this case and to instruct you on my decision. You must follow my instruction in considering both infringement and invalidity issues.

One limit on the doctrine of equivalents occurs as the result of changes to the patent claims or arguments that the patent owner made in order to obtain his or her patent. A patent owner may not include within the patent claims [products or processes] that he or she gave up in order to obtain his or her patent.

In this case, the following limits apply to the claims of the _____ patent.

[Court to supply any prosecution history estoppel.]

Another limit on the doctrine of equivalents occurs when the patent specification describes a specific role or function for a claim limitation. When this occurs, any equivalent structure must fill substantially the same role as that described in the patent specification for that limitation. In this case, this limit applies as follows:

[Court to supply any such limit.]

NOTE

As the Supreme Court has noted, "the doctrine of equivalents, when applied broadly, conflicts with the definitional and public-notice functions of the statutory claiming requirement." *Warner-Jenkinson Co. v. Hilton Davis Chem. Co.*, 520 U.S. 17, 29 (1997). A number of doctrines apply to limit the scope of the doctrine of equivalents and thus preserve the public notice function of claims. Application of these doctrines is a matter of law for the Court. *See K-2 Corp. v. Salomon S.A.*, 191 F.3d 1356, 1367 (Fed. Cir. 1999). Thus, the Court must determine the limitations that apply, and instruct the jury as to these limitations. To avoid jury confusion, we have omitted any discussion in these instructions about how these limiting doctrines are applied.

The major doctrines that apply to limit application of the doctrine of equivalents include prosecution history estoppel, the "all elements rule," limits based on the role set out in the patent specification for a particular claim limitation, and limits based on subject matter that is disclosed in a patent specification but not claimed.

Prosecution History Estoppel

It is well settled that a patent owner's actions during prosecution in obtaining allowance of patent claims may limit the range of equivalents to which the claims are entitled. *Festo Corp.* v. *Shoketsu Kinzoku Kogyo Kabushiki Co.*, 535 U.S. 722, 739, 122 S.Ct. 1831, 1841 (2002) ("[T]he doctrine of equivalents and the rule of prosecution history estoppel are settled law.") The doctrine of prosecution history estoppel prevents claims from being expanded under the doctrine of equivalents to encompass subject matter given up during prosecution. Prosecution history estoppel may be based on claim amendments or arguments made in support of patentability.

In *Festo Corp.* v. *Shoketsu Kinzoku Kogyo Kabushiki Co.*, 234 F.3d 558, 564 (Fed. Cir. 2000), the Federal Circuit, sitting *en banc*, held that any narrowing amendment made for any reason related to the statutory requirements for patentability (*e.g.*, 35 U.S.C. §§ 101, 102, 103 and 112) will create a prosecution history estoppel. An estoppel will also arise when a narrowing amendment was made voluntarily, or if the reason for the amendment is ambiguous. *Id.* at 568, 578; *see also Festo*, 344 F.3d 1359, 1366–7 (Fed. Cir. 2003).

The Federal Circuit further held that when a claim amendment creates a prosecution history estoppel with respect to a claim limitation, that limitation is entitled to no range of equivalents. The Court reasoned that the prior "flexible bar" approach for determining the range of equivalents that the patent owner had surrendered during prosecution had proven unworkable. In particular, the public notice function of patent claims was undermined because the flexible bar approach made the determination of the scope of any estoppel extremely difficult to predict. *Id*. at 575.

The Supreme Court reversed the Federal Circuit's decision in this regard in favor of a more flexible approach for determining equivalents in light of an estoppel. The Supreme Court noted that the Federal Circuit's decision over-turned well-settled law and ran the risk of "destroying the legitimate expectations of inventors" who prosecute patents in light of case law. *Festo*, 122 S.Ct. at 1841.

In determining the range of equivalents for an amended claim limitation, the Supreme Court held that if a patent owner makes a narrowing amendment for a reason related to patentability, it will be presumed that such an amendment is "a general disclaimer of territory between the original claim and the amended claim." *Id*. at 1842. It is then the patent owner's burden to overcome the presumption by showing that: (1) the equivalent would have been unforeseeable at the time of the amendment; (2) the rationale underlying the amendment bore no more than a tangential relation to the equivalent in question; or (3) there was some other reason suggesting that the patentee could not reasonably be expected to have described the insubstantial substitute in question. *Id*.

On remand from the Supreme Court, the Federal Circuit, sitting *en banc*, provided additional guidance regarding the three ways in which a patent owner may overcome the presumption. *Festo*, 344 F.3d 1359. The Federal Circuit explained that with respect to the first way:

> This criterion presents an objective inquiry, asking whether the alleged equivalent would have been unforeseeable to one of ordinary skill in the art at the time of the amendment. Usually, if the alleged equivalent represents later-developed technology (*e.g.*, transistors in relation to vacuum tubes, or Velcro® in relation to fasteners) or technology that was not known in the relevant art, then it would not have been foreseeable. In contrast, old technology, while not always foreseeable, would more likely have been foreseeable. Indeed, if the alleged equivalent were known

in the prior art in the field of the invention, it certainly should have been foreseeable at the time of the amendment.

Id. at 1369.

With respect to the second way, the Federal Circuit stated:

[T]his criterion asks whether the reason for the narrowing amendment was peripheral, or not directly relevant, to the alleged equivalent. Although we cannot anticipate the instances of mere tangentialness that may arise, we can say that an amendment made to avoid prior art that contains the equivalent in question is not tangential; it is central to allowance of the claim.

Id.

Finally, with respect to the third way, the Court stated:

[T]he third criterion may be satisfied when there was some reason, such as the shortcomings of language, why the patentee was prevented from describing the alleged equivalent when it narrowed the claim. When at all possible, determination of the third rebuttal criterion should also be limited to the prosecution history record. For example, as we recently held in *Pioneer Magnetics, Inc. v. Micro Linear Corp.*, 330 F.3d 1352 (Fed. Cir. 2003), a patentee may not rely on the third rebuttal criterion if the alleged equivalent is in the prior art, for then "there can be no other reason the patentee could not have described the substitute in question."

Id. at 1370.

The *en banc* Court also made clear that the question of rebuttal, like all questions relating to the application and scope of prosecution history estoppel, is a question of law for the court and not the jury. *Id.* at 1367.

An estoppel may also arise from arguments or statements made by a patent owner in support of patentability, even if the argument was not a direct response to a rejection of claims. *Texas Instruments* v. *United States Int'l Trade Comm'n*, 988 F.2d 1165, 1174 (Fed. Cir. 1993); *see also Ekchian* v. *Home Depot*, 104 F.3d 1299, 1304 (Fed. Cir. 1997) ("arguments in an [Information Disclosure Statement] can create an estoppel"); *Bayer AG* v. *Elan Pharm. Research Corp.*, 212 F.3d 1241, 1252

(Fed. Cir. 2000) (an applicant's repeated statements regarding unique and unexpected results limited the range of equivalents to [products/processes] that achieved those results).

The All Elements Rule

The "all elements rule" preserves the public notice function of claims by preventing the doctrine of equivalents from expanding claims so as effectively to eliminate a claim limitation. *See Warner-Jenkinson, supra*, 520 U.S. at 29. Thus, where a claim limitation is absent from an accused product or process, there can be no infringement under the doctrine of equivalents. *See, e.g., Telemac Cellular Corp.* v. *Topp Telecom, Inc.*, 247 F.3d 1316 (Fed. Cir. 2001); *Zodiac Pool Care, Inc.* v. *Hoffinger Indus., Inc.*, 206 F.3d 1408, 1416 (Fed. Cir. 2000).

Defined Role for Claim Limitations

Another limitation on the range of equivalents to which a patent claim is entitled arises when the patent specification describes a specific role or function for a claim limitation. In this situation, any equivalent structure must serve substantially the same role or function as described in the specification.

In *Vehicular Techs. Corp.* v. *Titan Wheel Int'l, Inc.*, 212 F.3d 1377 (Fed. Cir. 2000), the claim in dispute required two concentric springs. The patent specification stated that the springs enhanced the system's reliability because the second spring served as a back-up for the first spring. In affirming the district court's holding of non-infringement, the Federal Circuit held that the accused device's allegedly equivalent element did not perform the "back-up" function referred to in the patent specification. The Court explained that "an accused device which does not perform this central function could, rarely, if ever, be considered to be insubstantially changed from the claimed invention." *Id*. at 1382.

Unclaimed Subject Matter

Another limitation on the doctrine of equivalents was recognized by the Federal Circuit in *Maxwell* v. *J. Baker, Inc.*, 86 F.3d 1098 (Fed. Cir. 1996). In that case, the Court held that subject matter that is disclosed but not claimed in a patent cannot be included within the range of equivalents to which the patent claims are entitled. The Federal Circuit took a different view, however, in *YBM Magnex, Inc.* v. *Int'l Trade Comm'n*, 145 F.3d 1317 (Fed. Cir. 1998), where the Court held that disclosed but unclaimed subject matter may fall within the claims' range of equivalents.

The Federal Circuit resolved the apparent conflict in *Johnson & Johnston Associates* v. *R.E. Service Co.*, 285 F.3d 1046 (Fed. Cir. 2002) (*en banc*). The *en banc* court overruled *YBM Magnex* in favor of the rule in Maxwell holding that "when a patent drafter discloses but declines to claim subject matter, . . . this action dedicates that unclaimed subject matter to the public." *Id.* at 1054. As a result, such subject matter would not fall within the patent claims' range of equivalents.

AUTHORITIES

Festo Corp. v. *Shoketsu Kinzoku Kogyo Kabushiki Co.*, 535 U.S. 722, 122 S.Ct. 1831 (2002); *Warner-Jenkinson Co.* v. *Hilton Davis Chem. Co.*, 520 U.S. 17, 29 (1997); *Festo Corp.* v. *Shoketsu Kinzoku Kogyo Kabushiki Co.*, 344 F.3d 1359 (Fed. Cir. 2003); *Pioneer Magnetics, Inc.* v. *Micro Linear Corp.*, 330 F.3d 1352 (Fed. Cir. 2003); *Schwing GMBH* v. *Putzmeister Aktiengesellschaft*, 305 F.3d 1318 (Fed. Cir. 2002); *Johnson & Johnston Associates* v. *R.E. Service Co.*, 285 F.3d 1046 (Fed. Cir. 2002) (*en banc*); *Smith & Nephew, Inc.* v. *Ethicon, Inc.*, 276 F.3d 1304, 1311; *Bell Atlantic Network Servs., Inc.* v. *Covad Communications Group, Inc.*, 262 F.3d 1258, 1279 (Fed. Cir. 2001); *Mycogen Plant Sci., Inc.* v. *Monsanto Co.*, 252 F.3d 1306, 1320 (Fed. Cir. 2001); *Telemac Cellular Corp.* v. *Topp Telecom, Inc.*, 247 F.3d 1316 (Fed. Cir. 2001); *Forest Labs.* v. *Abbott Labs.*, 239 F.3d 1305, 1314 (Fed. Cir. 2001); *Biovail Corp.* v. *Andrx Pharms., Inc.*, 239 F.3d 1297, 1301–02 (Fed. Cir. 2001); *Litton Sys., Inc.* v. *Honeywell Inc.*, 238 F.3d 1376, 1380 (Fed. Cir. 2001); *Johnson & Johnston Associates, Inc.* v. *R.E. Service Co.*, 238 F.3d 1347 (Fed. Cir. 2001); *Pioneer Magnetics, Inc.* v. *Micro Linear Corp.*, 238 F.3d 1341, 1344 (Fed. Cir. 2001); *Festo Corp.* v. *Shoketsu Kinzoku Kogyo Kabushiki Co.*, 234 F.3d 558 (Fed. Cir. 2000) (*en banc*); *Moore U.S.A., Inc.* v.

Standard Register Co., 229 F.3d 1091, 1106 (Fed. Cir. 2000); *Vehicular Techs. Corp.* v. *Titan Wheel Int'l, Inc.*, 212 F.3d 1377, 1381–83 (Fed. Cir. 2000); *Bayer AG* v. *Elan Pharm. Research Corp.*, 212 F.3d 1241, 1251–54 (Fed. Cir. 2000); *Zodiac Pool Care, Inc.* v. *Hoffinger Indus., Inc.*, 206 F.3d 1408, 1416 (Fed. Cir. 2000); *K-2 Corp.* v. *Salomon S.A.*, 191 F.3d 1356, 1366–68 (Fed. Cir. 1999); *Tronzo* v. *Biomet, Inc.*, 156 F.3d 1154, 1160 (Fed. Cir. 1998); *YBM Magnex, Inc.* v. *Int'l Trade Comm'n*, 145 F.3d 1317, 1320–22 (Fed. Cir. 1998); *Gentry Gallery, Inc.* v. *Berkline Corp.*, 134 F.3d 1473, 1477 (Fed. Cir. 1998); *Sage Prods., Inc.* v. *Devon Indus., Inc.*, 126 F.3d 1420, 1423 (Fed. Cir. 1997); *Ekchian* v. *Home Depot, Inc.*, 104 F.3d 1299, 1303–04 (Fed. Cir. 1997); *Cole* v. *Kimberly-Clark Corp.*, 102 F.3d 524, 532 (Fed. Cir. 1996); *Applied Materials, Inc.* v. *Advanced Semiconductor Materials Am., Inc.*, 98 F.3d 1563, 1573–74 (Fed. Cir. 1996); *Maxwell* v. *J. Baker, Inc.*, 86 F.3d 1098, 1106–08 (Fed. Cir. 1996); *Texas Instruments* v. *United States Int'l Trade Comm'n*, 988 F.2d 1165, 1174 (Fed. Cir. 1993); *Unique Concepts, Inc.* v. *Brown*, 939 F.2d 1558, 1563–64 (Fed. Cir. 1991).

7.5 Infringement—Means-plus-Function Claim Limitations

As I told you, a means-plus-function claim limitation describes a means for performing a particular function. To prove that an accused product includes a structure that is covered by a means-plus-function limitation, a patent owner must prove two things by the more probable than not standard: first, that the accused product contains a structure that performs the identical function to the function recited in the means-plus-function limitation; and second, that the structure of the accused product that performs that function is either identical or equivalent to the corresponding structure disclosed in the patent specification.

Whether or not the structure of the accused product is equivalent to the structure disclosed in the patent is decided from the perspective of a person of ordinary skill in the field of the invention. A person of ordinary skill is a person of average education and training in the field. A structure is equivalent if such an ordinary skilled person would consider the differences between the accused structure and the structure in the patent to be insubstantial.

One way of determining whether the structure of the accused product is equivalent to the structure disclosed in the specification is to determine whether or not persons of ordinary skill in the field of the invention believe that the structure disclosed in the specification and the structure of the accused product are interchangeable. Another way is to determine whether or not the accused structure performs the identical function, in substantially the same way, to achieve substantially the same result, as the structure disclosed in the specification.

Let's go back to our example of the claim reciting three limitations—first, a tabletop, second, legs and third, a means for securing the legs to the tabletop. The third limitation is the means-plus-function portion of the claim. The patent specification in our example discloses glue to secure the legs to the tabletop. Let's assume that the accused device uses nails.

They both perform the claimed function of securing the legs to the tabletop. The fact that nails and glue are different does not mean that, under the patent laws, they may not be equivalent. Whether or not they are equivalent depends on such things as whether the glue is important to the invention claimed in the patent, whether those skilled in the art of table-making would consider the glue and nails to be interchangeable, and whether in the patent or prosecution history the two are referred to as equivalent.

NOTE

This instruction should be used when infringement under the doctrine of equivalents is not an issue with respect to a means-plus-function limitation.

Determining whether or not a disclosed structure corresponds to the function recited in a means-plus-function limitation involves a question of law for the court. *IMS Tech.* v. *Haas Automation, Inc.*, 206 F.3d 1422, 1436 (Fed. Cir. 2000). In setting forth the court's claim construction (*see* Instruction 6.6), the court should instruct the jury on the structure disclosed in the patent specification that corresponds to the means-plus-function limitation. The court's focus should be, not on whether or not the disclosed structure can perform the claimed function, but rather, on whether or not the patent specification indicates to one of skill in the art that the disclosed structure can perform the claimed function. *See Medtronic, Inc.* v. *Advanced Cardiovascular Sys., Inc.*, 248 F.3d 1303, 1311 (Fed. Cir. 2001) ("structure disclosed in the specification is 'corresponding' structure only if the specification or prosecution history clearly links or associates that structure to the function recited in the claims (citation omitted).") Thus, even if the patent specification discloses multiple structures that are capable of performing the claimed function, it may be appropriate for a court to identify only one of these structures as the "corresponding structure." *Id.* at 1315.

Once the court instructs the jury as to the structure disclosed in the patent specification that corresponds to a means-plus-function limitation, the jury must determine whether or not the accused product contains an element that falls within the scope of the means-plus-function limitation. That is, the jury must answer the question "does the accused device contain the structure in the specification corresponding to the means-plus-function limitation or its equivalents?" Structures are equivalent if one of skill in the art would consider the differences between them to be insubstantial. *See IMS Tech. v. Haas Automation, Inc.*, 206 F.3d 1422, 1436 (Fed. Cir. 2000). Courts have recognized two ways for determining whether or not such differences are insubstantial: (1) whether or not the accused product performs the identical function in substantially the same way to achieve substantially the same result (*see IMS Tech.*, 206 F.3d at 1436); and (2) whether or not one of ordinary skill in the art would recognize the interchangeability of the element in the accused product and the disclosed structure (*see Chiuminatta Concrete Concepts, Inc. v. Cardinal Indus.*, 145 F.3d 1303, 1310 (Fed. Cir. 1998)).

In determining whether or not differences between the accused product and the disclosed structure are insubstantial, the disclosed structure must be considered as a whole. The Federal Circuit has made it clear that it is impermissible to engage in a component-by-component analysis of the corresponding structure. *J&M Corp. v. Harley-Davidson, Inc.*, 269 F.3d 1360, 1367 (Fed. Cir. 2001); *Odetics, Inc. v. Storage Tech. Corp.*, 185 F.3d 1259, 1268 (Fed. Cir. 1999); *Caterpillar Inc. v. Deere & Co.*, 224 F.3d 1374, 1380 (Fed. Cir. 2000) (reversing the district court's holding of non-infringement because the Court had impermissibly engaged in a component-by-component analysis).

As with other limitations, courts have considered the patent owner's actions during prosecution (*e.g.*, amendments or arguments) to limit the range of equivalents to which means-plus-function limitations are entitled. *See, e.g., Alpex Computer Corp. v. Nintendo Co.*, 102 F.3d 1214, 1221 (Fed. Cir. 1996). Also considered is the importance of the limitation to the claimed invention. *IMS*, 206 F.3d at 1436 ("[W]hen in a claimed 'means' limitation the disclosed physical structure is of little or no importance to the claimed invention, there may be a broader range of equivalent structures than if the physical characteristics of the structure are critical in performing the claimed function in the context of the claimed invention."). These types of considerations have not been included in the jury instructions and are left to the argument of counsel, if pertinent.

AUTHORITIES

35 U.S.C. § 112 ¶ 6 (1984); *J&M Corp.* v. *Harley-Davidson, Inc.*, 269 F.3d 1360, 1367 (Fed. Cir. 2001); *Medtronic, Inc.* v. *Advanced Cardiovascular Sys., Inc.*, 248 F.3d 1303, 1311 (Fed. Cir. 2001); *IMS Tech., Inc.* v. *Haas Automation, Inc.*, 206 F.3d 1422, 1435–37 (Fed. Cir. 2000); *Caterpillar Inc.* v. *Deere & Co.*, 224 F.3d 1374, 1380 (Fed. Cir. 2000); *Odetics, Inc.* v. *Storage Tech. Corp.*, 185 F.3d 1259, 1266–68 (Fed. Cir. 1999); *WMS Gaming Inc.* v. *Int'l Game Tech.*, 184 F.3d 1339, 1347–50 (Fed. Cir. 1999); *Al-Site Corp.* v. *VSI Int'l, Inc.*, 174 F.3d 1308, 1318–21 (Fed. Cir. 1999); *Chiuminatta Concrete Concepts, Inc.* v. *Cardinal Indus., Inc.*, 145 F.3d 1303, 1307–10 (Fed. Cir. 1998); *B. Braun Med. Inc.* v. *Abbott Labs.*, 124 F.3d 1419, 1424–25 (Fed. Cir. 1997); *Alpex Computer Corp.* v. *Nintendo Co.*, 102 F.3d 1214, 1221 (Fed. Cir. 1996).

7.6 Infringement—Means-plus-Function Claim Limitations

As I told you, a means-plus-function claim limitation describes a means for performing a particular function. A means-plus-function limitation may be present in an accused product literally or under the doctrine of equivalents.

To prove that an accused product includes a structure that is literally covered by a means-plus-function limitation, a patent owner must prove two things by the more probable than not standard. First, that the accused product contains a structure that performs the identical function to the function recited in the means-plus-function limitation. Second, that the structure of the accused product that performs that function is either identical or equivalent to the corresponding structure disclosed in the patent specification.

If the function performed by the structure is not identical to the function recited in the means-plus-function limitation, the patent owner may prove that the accused product is covered by the means-plus-function limitation under the doctrine of equivalents. To prove equivalents, the patent owner must prove, first, that the accused product contains a structure that performs an equivalent function to the one recited in the claim limitation, and second, that the structure that performs that function is identical or equivalent to the structure described in the patent specification.

Whether or not the structure or function of the accused product is equivalent to the structure disclosed in the patent and the function recited in the claims is decided from the perspective of a person of ordinary skill in the field of the invention. A person of ordinary skill is a person of average education and training in the field. A structure or function is equivalent if such an ordinary skilled person would consider the differences between the accused structure or function and the structure or function in the patent to be insubstantial.

One way of determining whether the structure of the accused product is equivalent to the structure disclosed in the specification is to determine whether or not persons of ordinary skill in the field of the invention believe that the structure disclosed in the specification and the structure of the accused product are interchangeable. Another way is to determine whether or not the accused structure performs substantially the same function, in substantially the same way, to achieve substantially the same result, as the structure disclosed in the specification.

Let's go back to our example of the claim reciting three limitations—first, a tabletop, second, legs and third, a means for securing the legs to the tabletop. The third limitation is the means-plus-function portion of the claim. The patent specification in our example discloses glue to secure the legs to the tabletop. Let's assume that the accused device uses nails. They both perform the claimed function of securing the legs to the tabletop. The fact that nails and glue are different does not mean that, under the patent laws, they may not be equivalent. Whether or not they are equivalent depends on such things as whether the glue is important to the invention claimed in the patent, whether those skilled in the art of table-making would consider the glue and nails to be interchangeable, and whether in the patent or prosecution history the two are referred to as equivalent.

[Recently, the Federal Circuit has applied a temporal approach to the infringement analysis of means-plus-function claims. The Court explained that:

> [A] structural equivalent under section 112 must have been available at the time of the issuance of the claim. An equivalent structure or act under section 112 cannot embrace technology developed after the issuance of the patent because the literal meaning of a claim is fixed upon issuance. An "after-arising equivalent" infringes, if at all, under the doctrine of equivalents.

Al-Site Corp. v. *VSI Int'l, Inc.,* **174 F.3d 1308, 1320 (Fed. Cir. 1999) (internal citations omitted);** *see also Chiuminatta Concrete Concepts, Inc.* v. *Cardinal Indus., Inc.,* **145 F.3d 1303, 1310 (Fed. Cir. 1998).**

Under those cases, include the following additional instruction]:

Equivalency is determined as of the issuance of the patent, in this case _____. In deciding whether or not a structure in [defendant's] product is included in the means-plus-function limitation of claims _____ of the _____ patent, you must first decide whether or not the technology used in the structure of [defendant's] product that relates to the means-plus-function limitation was known on the date the _____ patent issued. Under the patent laws, a structure that incorporates technology that was developed after the issuance of the patent cannot be literally included in the means-plus-function limitations of that patent.

Thus, if you find that the technology incorporated in the structure of [defendant's] product was developed after the _____ patent issued, then you can only consider whether or not the means-plus-function limitations of the _____ patent claims are included in [defendant's] product under the doctrine of equivalents.

NOTE

This instruction should be used instead of Instruction 7.5 when infringement under the doctrine of equivalents is an issue with respect to a means-plus-function limitation.

If there is no literal infringement of a means-plus-function limitation, there may nevertheless be infringement under the doctrine of equivalents. The Federal Circuit has recognized that there is substantial overlap between § 112, ¶ 6 equivalents and the doctrine of equivalents (*see IMS Tech.* v. *Haas Automation, Inc.,* 206 F.3d 1422, 1436 (Fed. Cir. 2000)) and some notable differences. Equivalents under § 112, ¶ 6 requires that the accused device perform the *identical* function to that specified in the means-plus-function limitation, in substantially the same way to achieve substantially the same result. In contrast, equivalence under the doctrine of equivalents requires only that the accused device perform *substantially the same* function in substantially the same way to achieve substantially the same result. *See Chiuminatta Concrete Concepts, Inc.* v. *Cardinal Indus.*, 145 F.3d 1303, 1310 (Fed. Cir. 1998).

AUTHORITIES

35 U.S.C. § 112 ¶ 6 (1984); *IMS Tech., Inc.* v. *Haas Automation, Inc.*, 206 F.3d 1422, 1435–37 (Fed. Cir. 2000); *Caterpillar Inc.* v. *Deere & Co.*, 224 F.3d 1374, 1380 (Fed. Cir. 2000); *Odetics, Inc.* v. *Storage Tech. Corp.*, 185 F.3d 1259, 1266–68 (Fed. Cir. 1999); *WMS Gaming Inc.* v. *Int'l Game Tech.*, 184 F.3d 1339, 1347–50 (Fed. Cir. 1999); *Al-Site Corp.* v. *VSI Int'l, Inc.*, 174 F.3d 1308, 1318–21 (Fed. Cir. 1999); *Chiuminatta Concrete Concepts, Inc.* v. *Cardinal Indus., Inc.*, 145 F.3d 1303, 1307–10 (Fed. Cir. 1998); *B. Braun Med. Inc.* v. *Abbott Labs.*, 124 F.3d 1419, 1424–25 (Fed. Cir. 1997).

7.7   Determination of Infringement

Taking each claim of the _____ patent separately, if you find that [plaintiff] has proved that it is more probable than not that each and every limitation of the claim is present, either literally or under the doctrine of equivalents, in [defendant's] accused [product or process], then you must find that [defendant's] [product or process] infringes that claim.

7.8 The Experimental Use Exception

The patent law regards the use of a [product or process] for an experimental purpose differently from use for a commercial purpose. Thus, the law provides an exception to infringement when the accused [product or process] was used strictly for experimental purposes. This is known as the "experimental use exception."

The experimental use exception permits someone to use a [product or process] covered by a patent without the patent owner's permission, as long as the use is merely for philosophical experiments, or to determine whether a [product or process] will work for its intended purpose. Such uses do not infringe a patent. Where, however, a use is in connection with a commercial purpose, the experimental use exception does not apply and the use will be an infringement.

[Defendant] asserts that its use of the accused [product or process] falls within the experimental use exception and, therefore, does not infringe claims _____ of the _____ patent. If you find that [defendant's] use of the accused [product or process] was-merely for philosophical purposes, or to determine whether the accused [product or process] will work for its intended purpose, then you should find [defendant's] use to be experimental, and thus not an infringement of the _____ patent. If, however, you find that [defendant's] use of the accused [product or process] was in connection with a commercial purpose of [defendant], then you should find that use not to have been experimental. In that case, the experimental use exception to infringement will not apply.

NOTE

The experimental use exception to infringement permits a third party to use a patented invention if that use is strictly experimental. The vitality of the experimental use exception was recently recognized by the Federal Circuit in *Embrex, Inc. v. Serv. Eng'g Corp.*, 216 F.3d 1343 (Fed. Cir. 2000), although the Court rejected application of the defense to the facts of that particular case. The Court emphasized that this defense has consistently been narrowly applied.

The defense does not, however, have the uniform support of the Federal Circuit bench. In a concurring opinion in *Embrex*, Judge Rader called for an end to the experimental use exception. Judge Rader suggested that the Patent Act, as well as the Supreme Court's decision in *Warner-Jenkinson* v. *Hilton Davis*, 520 U.S. 17, 36 (1997), which held that intent plays no role in an infringement analysis, leave no room for the experimental use defense.

AUTHORITIES

35 U.S.C. § 271(e)(1) (Supp. 2001); *Embrex, Inc.* v. *Serv. Eng'g Corp.*, 216 F.3d 1343, 1349 (Fed. Cir. 2000); *Roche Prods., Inc.* v. *Bolar Pharm. Co.*, 733 F.2d 858 (Fed. Cir. 1984).

7.9　　　Infringement of Product-by-Process Claims

[There is a split in authority in the Court of Appeals for the Federal Circuit regarding infringement of product-by-process claims. Under *Scripps Clinic & Research Found.* v. *Genentech Inc.*, 927 F.2d 1565 (Fed. Cir. 1991), the following jury instruction should be used]:

As I told you, a product-by-process claim describes a product in terms of the process by which it is made. In order for a product to infringe a product-by-process claim, the accused product must be the same as, or equivalent to, the product described in the claim. It is not necessary, however, that the product actually be produced using the method described in the claim.

Claims _____ of the _____ patent are product-by-process claims. If you find that [plaintiff] has proved that it is more probable than not that [defendant's] [product] is the same as, or equivalent to, the product described in the claims, then you must find that [defendant's] product infringes the claims.

[Under *Atl. Thermoplastics Co.* v. *Faytex Corp.*, 970 F.2d 834 (Fed. Cir. 1992), the following jury instruction should be used]:

As I told you, a product-by-process claim describes a product by the process by which it is made. In order for a product to infringe a product-by-process claim, it must be made by the same or an equivalent process to the one recited in the claim.

Claims _____ of the _____ patent are product-by-process claims. If you find that [plaintiff] has proved that it is more probable than not that [defendant's] product is the same as, or equivalent to, the product described in the claims, and was made by the same process as the process recited in the claims, then you must find that [defendant's] product infringes those claims.

NOTE

Product-by-process claims have their genesis in "the need to enable an applicant to claim an otherwise patentable product that resists definition by other than the process by which it is made." *In re Thorpe*, 777 F.2d 695, 697 (Fed. Cir. 1985). Patentability of such claims, however, is based on the product itself, without resort to the process limitations. *See, e.g., id.*

In 1991, the Federal Circuit in *Scripps Clinic & Research Found. v. Genentech Inc.*, 927 F.2d 1565 (Fed. Cir. 1991), held that infringement of product-by-process claims, like patentability, is determined solely by the patentability of the claimed product:

> Since claims must be construed the same way for validity and for infringement, the correct reading of product-by-process claims is that they are not limited to product[s] prepared by the process set forth in the claims.

Id. at 1583.

A year later, Judge Rader, writing for the panel in *Atl. Thermoplastics Co. v. Faytex Corp.*, 970 F.2d 834 (Fed. Cir. 1992), disagreed with the *Scripps* panel, holding that "process terms in product-by-process claims serve as limitations in determining infringement." *Id.* at 846–47.

Citing to Supreme Court and Court of Customs and Patent Appeal (a predecessor court to the Federal Circuit) decisions dating back to the 1800's, the *Atl. Thermoplastics* Court concluded that the process recited in a product-by-process claim did limit and define the claimed product, even though patentability was based on the product. *Id.* at 838–46. The Court noted that patent claims have historically been treated differently for patentability in Patent Office proceedings and for validity and infringement in a litigation context. The Court held that ignoring the process limitations in product-by-process claims would conflict with the long-standing principle that "infringement requires the presence of every claim limitation or its equivalent." *Id.* at 846.

The opportunity arose for the Federal Circuit to resolve the conflict between the *Scripps* and *Atl. Thermoplastics* decisions when the patent owner in *Atl. Thermoplastics* filed a petition for rehearing *en banc*. A majority of Federal Circuit judges, however, denied the petition. *Atl. Thermoplastics Co.* v. *Faytex Corp.*, 974 F.2d 1279 (Fed. Cir. 1992). In scathing dissents, Judges Rich, Newman and Lourie criticized the *Atl. Thermoplastics* panel decision as unnecessary and incorrect on the law.

Judge Newman distinguished "true" product-by-process claims, such as the complex biological compositions of the *Scripps* case, which were directed to novel and unobvious products that were "not capable of independent definition," from "product of the process" claims, such as the shoe innersole claims of the *Atl. Thermoplastics* case, which were old and patentable only because of the patentability of the recited process. *Id.* at 1282–84. According to Judge Newman, courts have historically refused to limit the former type of claims to the recited process limitations, whereas the latter type of claims were necessarily so limited. *Id.* at 1283. Judge Newman concluded:

> The experience of technological innovation, and today's dramatic discoveries involving biological products, show the continuing role of the ["true" product-by-process] class of claim. It is inappropriate for a panel of this court, on the basis of a shoe innersole, to decide that the discoverer of a novel and unobvious biological product whose structure is not objectively known can not claim that product *per se*.

Id. at 1298.

The division of the Federal Circuit on this point is echoed in the split among the district courts that have considered the issue after *Atl. Thermoplastics*. *See Trustees of Columbia Univ.* v. *Roche Diagnostics GmbH*, 126 F. Supp.2d 16, 32 (D. Mass. 2000) (following *Scripps*); *Dekalb Genetics Corp.* v. *Northrup King Co.*, No. 96C 501169, 1997 WL 587492 at *2 (N.D. Ill. Aug. 14, 1997) (following *Scripps*); *Tropix, Inc.* v. *Lumigen, Inc.*, 825 F. Supp. 7, 10 (D. Mass. 1993) (following *Atl. Thermoplastics*).

AUTHORITIES

Vanguard Prods. Corp. v. *Parker Hannifin Corp.*, 234 F.3d 1370, 1372–73 (Fed. Cir. 2000); *Exxon Chem. Patents, Inc.* v. *Lubrizol*

Corp., 64 F.3d 1553, 1557–58 (Fed. Cir. 1995); *Mentor Corp. v. Colopast, Inc.*, 998 F.2d 992, 997 (Fed. Cir. 1993); *Atl. Thermoplastics Co. v. Faytex Corp.*, 970 F.2d 834, 837 (Fed. Cir. 1992) *reh'g en banc denied*, 974 F.2d 1279 (Fed. Cir. 1992); *Scripps Clinic & Research Found. v. Genentech, Inc.*, 927 F.2d 1565 (Fed. Cir. 1991); *In re Thorpe*, 777 F.2d 695, 697 (Fed. Cir. 1985); *Trustees of Columbia Univ. v. Roche Diagnostics GmbH*, 126 F. Supp.2d 16, 32 (D. Mass. 2000); *Dekalb Genetics Corp. v. Northrup King Co.*, No. 96C 501169, 1997 WL 587492 at *2 (N.D. Ill. Aug. 14, 1997); *Tropix, Inc. v. Lumigen, Inc.*, 825 F. Supp. 7, 10 (D. Mass. 1993).

7.10   Infringement of Dependent Claims

My instructions on infringement so far have related to independent claims. As I told you, the _____ patent also contains dependent claims. A dependent claim includes each of the limitations of the independent claim to which it refers, plus additional elements.

If you find that independent claim _____ of the _____ patent has been infringed, you must separately determine whether dependent claim _____ has also been infringed. [If you find that the independent claims are not infringed, then you must also find that the dependent claims are not infringed.]

NOTE

The bracketed sentence describes the general rule that dependent claims cannot be infringed if the claims from which they depend are not infringed. *Wahpeton Canvas Co.* v. *Frontier, Inc.*, 870 F.2d 1546, 1552–53 n. 9 (Fed. Cir. 1989). An exception to this general rule may exist in the context of infringement under the doctrine of equivalents. If a finding of no infringement under the doctrine of equivalents of an independent claim is based upon limits to the range of equivalents imposed by the prior art, the dependent claims may nevertheless be infringed because "it does not automatically follow that the ranges of equivalents of these narrower [dependent] claims would encompass the prior art." *Wilson Sporting Goods Co.* v. *David Geoffrey & Assocs.*, 904 F.2d 677, 685–86 (Fed. Cir. 1990).

AUTHORITIES

Jeneric/Pentron, Inc. v. *Dillon Co.*, 205 F.3d 1377, 1383 (Fed. Cir. 2000); *Finnigan Corp.* v. *United States Int'l Trade Comm'n*, 180 F.3d 1354, 1364 (Fed. Cir. 1999); *Wilson Sporting Goods Co.* v. *David Geoffrey & Assocs.*, 904 F.2d 677, 685-86 (Fed. Cir. 1990); *Wahpeton Canvas Co.* v. *Frontier, Inc.*, 870 F.2d 1546, 1552–53 n.9 (Fed. Cir. 1989).

7.11 Infringement and Improvements to Patented Invention

[Defendant] has presented evidence that its [product or process] accused of infringement represents an improvement of the invention described in the _____ patent claims. Proof of this fact does not necessarily mean that the accused [product or process] does not infringe [plaintiff's] patent claims. The tests for infringement remain as I have instructed you. As long as you find that [defendant's] accused [product or process] includes all of the limitations of at least one of the _____ patent claims, either literally or under the doctrine of equivalents, then you must find that the _____ patent claims are infringed by [defendant's] accused [product or process], despite defendant's improvements.

NOTE

It is well settled that "an improvement upon a patented device does not necessarily avoid infringement." *Stiftung* v. *Reinshaw PLC*, 945 F.2d 1173, 1179 (Fed. Cir. 1991). Evidence that an accused infringer has obtained a patent on the accused product or process may, however, be relevant (although not dispositive) in determining whether or not the accused device is "insubstantially different" from the claimed invention and, therefore, infringes under the doctrine of equivalents. *See Nat'l Presto Indus., Inc.* v. *W. Bend, Co.,* 76 F.3d 1185, 1192 (Fed. Cir. 1996) ("the fact of separate patentability is relevant, and is entitled to due weight"); *see also Zygo Corp.* v. *Wyko Corp.,* 79 F.3d 1563 (Fed. Cir. 1996); *Hoechst Celanese Corp.* v. *BP Chems. Ltd.,* 78 F.3d 1575 (Fed. Cir. 1996).

AUTHORITIES

Nat'l Presto Indus., Inc. v. *W. Bend Co.,* 76 F.3d 1185, 1191–92 (Fed. Cir. 1996); *Zygo Corp.* v. *Wyko Corp.,* 79 F.3d 1563, 1570 (Fed. Cir. 1996); *Hoechst Celanese Corp.* v. *BP Chems. Ltd.,* 78 F.3d 1575, 1582 (Fed. Cir. 1996); *Stiftung* v. *Renishaw, PLC,*

945 F.2d 1173, 1179 (Fed. Cir. 1991); *Marsh-McBirney, Inc.* v. *Montedoro-Whitney Corp.*, 882 F.2d 498, 504 (Fed. Cir. 1989); *Atlas Powder Co.* v. *E. I. Du Pont de Nemours & Co.*, 750 F.2d 1569, 1580-81 (Fed. Cir. 1984).

7.12   Indirect Infringement

As I have told you, in addition to enforcing a patent against a direct infringer, a patent owner may also enforce the patent against indirect infringers. There are two types of indirect infringement: inducing infringement and contributory infringement. The act of encouraging or inducing others to infringe a patent is called "inducing infringement." The act of contributing to the infringement of others by, for example, supplying them with components used in the patented invention is called "contributory infringement."

There can be no indirect infringement unless someone is directly infringing the patent. Thus, in order to prove that [defendant] is inducing another person to infringe or contributing to the infringement of another, [plaintiff] must prove that it is more probable than not that the other person is directly infringing at least one claim of the patent.

In this case, [plaintiff] accuses [defendant] of [inducing or contributing to the] infringement of claims _____ of the _____ patent. [Plaintiff] must prove that it is more probable than not that [defendant] has [induced or contributed to the] infringement of any of these claims.

NOTE

Indirect infringement imposes patent infringement liability upon a third party who does not practice the claimed invention, but contributes to or aids in another's direct infringement. There are two types of indirect infringement—inducement to infringe and contributory infringement. 35 U.S.C. §§ 271(b) and (c) (1984 & Supp. 2001). These two types of indirect infringement are addressed in Instructions 7.12.1 and 7.12.2, which should be read only if applicable to the case at issue.

AUTHORITIES

Aro Mfg. Co. v. *Convertible Top Replacement Co.*, 365 U.S. 336, 340–41 (1961); *Arthur A. Collins, Inc.* v. *N. Telcom Ltd.*, 216 F.3d 1042, 1049 (Fed. Cir. 2000); *Porter* v. *Farmers Supply Serv., Inc.*, 790 F.2d 882, 884–86 (Fed. Cir. 1986).

7.12.1   Inducing Patent Infringement

A person induces patent infringement if he or she purposefully causes, urges or encourages another to infringe a patent. Inducing infringement cannot occur unintentionally. This is different from direct infringement, which, as I've told you, can occur unintentionally. In order to prove inducement, the patent owner must prove that it is more probable than not that the accused inducer knew of the patent and encouraged or instructed another person to [use a product or perform a process] in a manner that infringes the patent. The patent owner must also prove that it is more probable than not that the other person infringed the patent. A person can be an inducer even if he or she thought that what he or she was encouraging or instructing the other person to do was not an infringement.

[Plaintiff] asserts that [defendant] induced patent infringement. [Plaintiff] must prove four things by the more probable than not standard:

First, [defendant] encouraged or instructed another person how to [use a product or perform a process] in a manner that you, the jury, find infringes the _____ patent claims.

Second, [defendant] knew of the _____ patent.

Third, [defendant] knew or should have known that its encouragement or instructions would likely result in the other person doing that which you find to be an infringement of the _____ patent.

Fourth, the other person infringed the _____ patent.

If, and only if, you are persuaded of each of these four things may you find that [defendant] induced patent infringement.

NOTE

35 U.S.C. § 271(b) (1984) provides that "[w]hoever actively induces infringement of a patent shall be liable as an infringer." In *Hewlett-Packard Co. v. Bausch & Lomb Inc.*, 909 F.2d 1464, 1469 (Fed. Cir. 1990), the Federal Circuit held that in-

ducement to infringe requires a showing of "actual intent to cause the acts which constitute the infringement." Under the *Hewlett-Packard* analysis, the focus is on the actor's intent to cause the third party to act in a manner that is found to be a direct infringement, not the actor's subjective belief as to whether or not the third party will ultimately be found to infringe.

Three months after the Federal Circuit's decision in *Hewlett-Packard*, the Federal Circuit decided *Manville Sales Corp.* v. *Paramount Sys., Inc.*, 917 F.2d 544 (Fed. Cir. 1990). In that case, the Court held that inducing infringement under 35 U.S.C. § 271(b) requires that the alleged infringer: (1) intended to cause the acts that constitute infringement and (2) "knew or should have known that his actions would induce actual infringement." *Id.* at 553. The Court reversed the district court's holding of inducing infringement in part because of evidence that the accused infringer had relied in good faith on an opinion of counsel and, therefore, lacked the specific intent to induce infringement. *See also Micro Chem., Inc.* v. *Great Plains Chem. Co.*, 194 F.3d 1250, 1261 (Fed. Cir. 1999) (finding that defendant had taken "reasonable steps to avoid [inducing] infringement," including obtaining an opinion of counsel).

The *Manville* decision has sparked some debate as to whether or not there is an opinion of counsel defense to infringement under § 271(b). *See* Michael N. Rader, *Toward a Coherent Law of Inducement to Infringe: Why the Federal Circuit Should Adopt the Hewlett-Packard Standard for Intent Under § 271(b)*, 10 Fed. Cir. B.J. (2000). Such a defense appears improperly to merge the requirements of § 271(b), as set forth in *Hewlett-Packard*, with the willful infringement standard, which recognizes the existence of an opinion of counsel as a defense to willful infringement. Some district courts have criticized *Manville* and held that a specific intent to infringe is not a necessary element of inducement to infringe. *See CVI/Beta Ventures, Inc.* v. *Tura LP*, 905 F. Supp. 1171, 1195 (E.D.N.Y. 1995), *rev'd in part, vacated in part*, 112 F.3d 1146 (Fed. Cir. 1997); *Curtis Mfg. Co.* v. *Plasti-Clip Corp.*, 888 F. Supp. 1212, 1224 (D.N.H. 1994);

Symbol Techs., Inc. v. *Metrologic Instruments,* 771 F. Supp. 1390, 1405 (D.N.J. 1991).

AUTHORITIES

35 U.S.C. § 271(b) (1984); *Moba, B.V.* v. *Diamond Automation, Inc.,* 325 F.3d 1306, 1318 (Fed. Cir. 2003); *Micro Chem., Inc.* v. *Great Plains Chem. Co.,* 194 F.3d 1250, 1261 (Fed. Cir. 1999); *Chiuminatta Concrete Concepts, Inc.* v. *Cardinal Indus., Inc.,* 145 F.3d 1303, 1311–12 (Fed. Cir. 1998); *Insituform Techs., Inc.* v. *Cat Contracting, Inc.,* 161 F.3d 688, 695 (Fed. Cir. 1998); *Carborundum Co.* v. *Molten Metal Equip. Innovations, Inc.,* 72 F.3d 872, 876 n.4 (Fed. Cir. 1995); *Joy Techs., Inc.* v. *Flakt, Inc.,* 6 F.3d 770, 774–76 (Fed. Cir. 1993); *Manville Sales Corp.* v. *Paramount Sys., Inc.,* 917 F.2d 544, 553–54 (Fed. Cir. 1990); *Hewlett-Packard Co.* v. *Bausch & Lomb Inc.,* 909 F.2d 1464, 1468–69 (Fed. Cir. 1990).

7.12.2   Contributory Infringement

Contributory infringement can occur when a supplier provides a part or a component to another for use in a patented product or machine, or in a patented process. In order for there to be contributory infringement, the person who received the component must infringe the patent. The component must also have certain characteristics. First, the component must be a material part of the invention. Second, the component must be especially made or adapted for use in a manner that infringes the patent, and the supplier must know that the component was especially made for that use. Third, the component must not have a substantial use that does not infringe the patent. A component that has a number of non-infringing uses is often referred to as a staple or commodity article. Providing such a staple or commodity article is not contributory infringement, even if the person to whom the article was supplied uses it in an infringing manner.

In this case, [plaintiff] asserts that [defendant's] selling or supplying _____ is contributing to the infringement of claims _____ of the _____ patent. In order to establish that [defendant] has contributorily infringed those claims, [plaintiff] must prove five things by the more probable than not standard:

First, [defendant] knew of the patent.

Second, _____ is a material component of the claimed invention and [defendant] sold or supplied that component.

Third, [defendant] knew that the intended use of the product would infringe the patent.

Fourth, the component is not a staple or commodity article.

Fifth, the component was actually used in a manner that you find infringes the patent.

NOTE

35 U.S.C. § 271(c) (2001) states that:

> Whoever offers to sell or sells within the United States or imports into the United States a component of a patented machine, man-

ufacture, combination or composition, or a material or apparatus for use in practicing a patented process, constituting a material part of the invention, knowing the same to be especially made or especially adapted for use in an infringement of such patent, and not a staple article or commodity of commerce suitable for substantial noninfringing use, shall be liable as a contributory infringer.

The Federal Circuit has consistently construed § 271(c) to require that the accused infringer know that the intended use of the product will infringe a known patent. The question of whether or not the presence of an opinion of counsel, as discussed in *Manville Sales*, 917 F.2d 544, regarding 35 U.S.C. § 271(b), would also be a defense to contributory infringement under § 271(c) has yet to be addressed by the Court.

AUTHORITIES

35 U.S.C. § 271(c) (Supp. 2001); *Aro Mfg. Co. v. Convertible Top Replacement Co.*, 377 U.S. 476 (1964); *Serrano v. Telular Corp.*, 111 F.3d 1578, 1583–84 (Fed. Cir. 1997); *Sage Prods., Inc. v. Devon Indus., Inc.*, 45 F.3d 1575, 1577 (Fed. Cir. 1995); *Carborundum Co. v. Molten Metal Equip. Innovations, Inc.*, 72 F.3d 872, 876 n.4 (Fed. Cir. 1995); *FMC Corp. v. Up-Right, Inc.*, 21 F.3d 1073, 1076 (Fed. Cir. 1994); *Joy Techs., Inc. v. Flakt, Inc.*, 6 F.3d 770, 774–76 (Fed. Cir. 1993); *Trell v. Marlee Elecs. Corp.*, 912 F.2d 1443, 1448 (Fed. Cir. 1990); *C.R. Bard, Inc. v. Advanced Cardiovascular Sys., Inc.*, 911 F.2d 670, 673 (Fed. Cir. 1990); *Hewlett-Packard Co. v. Bausch & Lomb Inc.*, 909 F.2d 1464, 1469 (Fed. Cir. 1990); *Hodosh v. Block Drug Co.*, 833 F.2d 1575, 1578–79 (Fed. Cir. 1987); *Preemption Devices, Inc. v. Minn. Mining & Mfg. Co.*, 803 F.2d 1170, 1174 (Fed. Cir. 1986).

Chapter Eight
Willful Infringement

8. Willful Infringement

[Plaintiff] also contends that [defendant] has willfully infringed the _____ patent claims. If you find on the basis of the evidence and the law as I have explained it, that [defendant] directly or indirectly infringes at least one claim of the _____ patent, you must then decide whether or not [defendant's] infringement was willful.

When a person becomes aware that a patent may have relevance to his or her activities, that person has a duty to exercise due care and to investigate whether or not his or her activities or proposed activities infringe any valid, enforceable claim of the patent. If that person did not do this and is found to have infringed any of the patent claims, then the infringement was willful.

The issue of willful infringement is relevant, not to your decision of whether or not there is infringement, but rather to the amount of damages to which [plaintiff] is entitled. A finding of willful infringement may, in certain circumstances, entitle the patent owner to increased damages. If you decide that [defendant] willfully infringed any of the _____ patent claims, then it is my job to decide whether or not to award increased damages to [plaintiff].

Although, as I explained before, [plaintiff] must prove infringement by the more probable than not standard, the burden of proving that the infringement was willful is the highly probable standard.

To establish willful infringement, [plaintiff] must prove two things by the highly probable standard. First, [plaintiff] must prove that [defendant] was aware of the _____ patent. Second, [plaintiff] must prove that [defendant] proceeded with the activities that are accused of infringement without a good faith belief that the patent was invalid, unenforceable and/or not infringed.

In determining whether or not [defendant] acted in good faith, you should consider all of the circumstances, including whether or not [defendant] obtained and followed the advice of a competent lawyer. The absence of a lawyer's opinion does not mean that infringement was willful, and you must not conclude that [defendant's] failure to obtain or rely on a lawyer's opinion means that any such opinion would have been unfavorable to [defendant]. However, the obtaining and following of a lawyer's advice may be evidence that infringement was not willful.

[In evaluating [defendant's] reliance on the advice of a lawyer, you should consider when [defendant] obtained the advice, the quality of the information [defendant] provided to the lawyer, the competence of the lawyer's opinion, and whether or not [defendant] relied upon the advice. Advice is competent if it was based upon a reasonable examination of the facts and law relating to validity, enforceability and/or infringement issues, consistent with the standards and practices generally followed by competent lawyers.]

Another factor you should consider in determining willfulness is whether or not, in designing the [product or process] accused of infringement, [defendant] copied the disclosures of the _____ patent, or whether or not [defendant] instead tried to "design around" the patent by designing a [product or process] that [defendant] believed did not infringe the patent claims. Evidence of copying a patent is evidence of willful infringement. On the other hand, evidence that [defendant] attempted to avoid infringement by designing around the patent claims, even if that attempt was unsuccessful, is evidence that the infringement was not willful.

The fact that you may have determined that [defendant] was wrong and that the _____ patent is infringed does not mean that [defendant's] infringement was willful. All that is required to avoid a finding of willful infringement is that [defendant] had a good faith belief that it did not infringe, that the patent was invalid, and/or that the patent was unenforceable and that [defendant's] belief was reasonable under all of the circumstances.

NOTE

The Federal Circuit has acknowledged that "[t]here are no hard and fast rules regarding a finding of willful [infringement]." *Grace, Inc.* v. *Binks Mfg. Co.*, 60 F.3d 785, 792 (Fed. Cir. 1995). Rather, the jury must take into consideration the totality of the circumstances. *Id.*

When performing a willful infringement analysis, the primary consideration is "whether the infringer, when it knew of the other's patent protection, investigated the scope of the patent and formed a good-faith belief that it was invalid or that it was not infringed." *Stryker Corp.* v. *Intermedics Orthopedics, Inc.*, 96 F.3d 1409, 1414 (Fed. Cir. 1996) (citation omitted). Accused infringers often rely on opinions of counsel as evidence of their good faith.

In an *en banc* decision rendered in September 2004, the Federal Circuit overruled precedent dating back to 1986 (*Kloster Speedsteel AB* v. *Crucible Inc.*, 193 F.2d 1565 (Fed. Cir. 1986); *see also Fromson* v. *Western Litho Plate & Supply Co.*, 853 F.2d 1568 (Fed. Cir. 1988)), and held that "no adverse inference that an opinion of counsel was or would have been unfavorable flows from an alleged infringer's failure to obtain or produce an exculpatory opinion of counsel." *Knorr-Bremse Systeme Fuer Nutzfahrzeuge GmbH* v. *Dana Corp.*, 2004 U.S. App. LEXIS 19185 (Fed. Cir. Sept. 13, 2004). The Court held that the drawing of an adverse inference would be inappropriate in situations where the infringer had either not received an opinion, or had received one but had declined to rely on it in the litigation.

In cases where infringers rely on opinions of counsel as evidence of their good faith, the Federal Circuit has considered a number of factors to determine whether or not an opinion of counsel was competent and, therefore, could provide a basis for the accused infringer's good-faith belief:

(1) Was the opinion written or oral? *Minnesota Mining & Mfg.* v. *Johnson and Johnson Orthopedics, Inc.*, 976 F.2d 1559, 1580 (Fed. Cir. 1992) (the Federal Circuit does not favor oral opinions).

(2) Did a patent attorney give the opinion? *Underwater Devices, Inc.* v. *Morrison-Knudsen, Co.*, 717 F.2d 1380, 1390 (Fed. Cir. 1983).

(3) Did in-house or outside counsel give the opinion? *Id.*

(4) Was the opinion conclusory in nature, or did it provide a thorough analysis of the relevant issues? *Read Corp.* v. *Portec, Inc.*, 970 F.2d 816, 830 (Fed. Cir. 1992).

The most important factor in determining whether or not the accused infringer's reliance on counsel's advice was sufficient is the presence or absence of objective evidence that would have alerted the infringer that the opinion was untrustworthy. *Read*, 970 F.2d at 829 ("A written opinion may be incompetent on its face by reason of its containing merely conclusory statements without discussion of facts or obviously presenting only a superficial or off-the-cuff analysis."). These factors may be addressed by counsel in opening or closing argument, as appropriate.

Once the jury has determined that an infringer acted willfully, the court must determine whether or not to increase damages, and the amount of any increase. *Id.* at 826. In making this determination, the Court may consider such evidence as:

(1) whether or not the infringer deliberately copied the patented invention;

(2) the infringer's behavior as a party to the litigation;

(3) the infringer's size and financial condition;

(4) the closeness of the case on infringement or invalidity;

(5) the duration of the infringing activity;

(6) actions taken by the infringer to avoid infringement; and

(7) whether or not the infringer attempted to conceal its infringement.

Id. at 827.

AUTHORITIES

35 U.S.C. § 284 (Supp. 2001); *Knorr-Bremse Systeme Fuer Nutz-fahrzeuge GmbH* v. *Dana Corp.*, 2004 U.S. App. LEXIS 19185 (Fed. Cir. Sept. 13, 2004); *WMS Gaming Inc.* v. *Int'l Game Tech.*, 184 F.3d 1339, 1354 (Fed. Cir. 1999); *Georgia-Pacific Corp.* v. *United States Gypsum Co.*, 195 F.3d 1322, 1334 (Fed. Cir. 1999); *John's Hopkins University* v. *Cellpro*, 152 F.3d 1342, 1363 (Fed. Cir. 1998); *Comark Comm, Inc.* v. *Harris Corp.*, 156 F.3d 1182, 1191 (Fed. Cir. 1998); *SRI Int'l, Inc.* v. *Advanced Tech. Labs.*, 127 F.3d 1462, 1465 (Fed. Cir. 1997); *Critikon, Inc.* v. *Becton Dickinson Vascular Access, Inc.*, 120 F.3d 1253, 1259-60 (Fed. Cir. 1997); *Nat'l Presto Indus.* v. *W. Bend Co.*, 76 F.3d 1185, 1192-93 (Fed. Cir. 1996); *Stryker Corp.* v. *Intermedics Orthopedics Inc.*, 96 F.3d 1409, 1414 (Fed. Cir. 1996); *Graco, Inc.* v. *Binks Mfg. Co.*, 60 F.3d 785, 792 (Fed. Cir. 1995); *Amsted Indus. Inc.* v. *Buckeye Steel Castings Co.*, 24 F.3d 178, 180 (Fed. Cir. 1994); *Westvaco Corp.* v. *Int'l Paper Co.*, 991 F.2d 735, 745 (Fed. Cir. 1993); *Minnesota Mining & Mfg.* v. *Johnson and Johnson Orthopedics, Inc.*, 976 F.2d 1559, 1580 (Fed. Cir. 1992); *Read Corp.* v. *Portec, Inc.*, 970 F.2d 816, 826-30 (Fed. Cir. 1992); *Ortho Pharm. Corp.* v. *Smith*, 959 F.2d 936, 944 (Fed. Cir. 1992); *Studiengesellschaft Kohle* v. Dart Indus., Inc., 862 F.2d 1564, 1579 (Fed. Cir. 1988); *Fromson* v. *Western Litho Plate & Supply Co.*, 853 F.2d 1568 (Fed. Cir. 1988); *Kloster Speedsteel AB* v. *Crucible Inc.*, 793 F.2d 1565 (Fed. Cir. 1986); *Underwater Devices, Inc.* v. *Morrison-Knudsen, Co.*, 717 F.2d 1380, 1390 (Fed. Cir. 1983).

Chapter Nine
Validity in General

9. Validity—in General

Only a valid patent may be infringed. For a patent to be valid, the invention claimed in the patent must be new, useful and nonobvious. A patent cannot take away from people their right to use what was known or what would have been obvious when the invention was made. The terms "new," "useful" and "nonobvious" have special meanings under the patent laws. I will explain these terms to you when we discuss [defendant's] grounds for asserting invalidity.

The invention claimed in a patent must also be adequately described. In return for the right to exclude others from making, using, selling or offering for sale the claimed invention, the patent owner must provide the public with a complete description in the patent of the invention and how to make and use it.

[Defendant] has challenged the validity of the _____ patent claims on a number of grounds. [Defendant] must prove that a patent claim is invalid by the highly probable standard.

I will now explain to you each of [defendant's] grounds for invalidity in detail. In making your determination as to invalidity, you should consider each claim separately.

NOTE

This instruction introduces the concept of patent validity and provides a brief, general description of the grounds for invalidating a patent claim. Patents are entitled to a presumption of validity. The presumption of validity, like all legal presumptions, is a procedural device. It "imposes on the party against whom it is directed the burden of going forward with evidence to rebut or meet the presumption." Fed. R. Evid. 301; *DMI, Inc.* v. *Deere & Co.*, 802 F.2d 421, 427 (Fed. Cir. 1986). As the Court of Appeals for the Federal Circuit has recognized, "the presumption is one of law, not fact, and does not constitute 'evidence' to be weighed against a challenger's evidence." *Avia Group Int'l, Inc.* v. *L.A. Gear Cal.*, 853 F.2d 1557, 1562 (Fed. Cir. 1988).

In light of the procedural role of the presumption of validity, instructing the jury on the presumption in addition to informing it of the clear and convincing burden of proof may cause jury confusion as to its role in deciding invalidity. This instruction, therefore, omits any reference to the presumption of validity.

It is axiomatic that each patent claim is considered a separate invention and, therefore, the validity or invalidity of each claim must be considered separately. 35 U.S.C. § 282 (Supp. 2001) ("[e]ach claim of a patent (whether in independent, dependent, or multiple dependent form) shall be presumed valid independently of the validity of other claims"). This is true for dependent claims as well as independent claims. *Id.* Where, however, the patent owner does not argue at trial for the validity of the dependent claims separately from the independent claims, the dependent claims will stand or fall with the independent claims from which they depend. *E.g., Enzo Biochem, Inc.* v. *Calgene, Inc.*, 188 F.3d 1362, 1377 (Fed. Cir. 1999).

9.1   Section 112 Defenses—Introduction

35 U.S.C. § 112, ¶ 1

35 U.S.C. § 112, ¶ 1 (1984) provides:

> The specification shall contain a written description of the invention, and of the manner and process of making and using it, in such full, clear, concise, and exact terms as to enable any person skilled in the art to which it pertains, or with which it is most nearly connected, to make and use the same, and shall set forth the best mode contemplated by the inventor of carrying out his invention.

This section contains three distinct requirements for a patent specification: (1) the specification must contain a "written description" of the claimed invention; (2) the specification must enable one of skill in the art to practice the claimed invention; and (3) the specification must set forth the inventor's best mode of practicing the claimed invention.

The first, or written description requirement, is satisfied when the patent specification and drawings describe the invention in such a manner that one of skill in the art would understand that the inventor was "in possession" of the claimed invention at the time the application was filed. *See Vas-Cath v. Mahurkar*, 935 F.2d 1555, 1563–64 (Fed. Cir. 1991). An inventor is said to be "in possession" of the claimed invention if the application describes all of the limitations of the patent claims. *Lockwood v. Am. Airlines, Inc.*, 107 F.3d 1565, 1572 (Fed. Cir. 1997). A written description will not pass § 112, ¶ 1 muster if a skilled person would only believe that the claimed invention was obvious in view of applicant's disclosure. Each limitation must be described. *Id.*

The second requirement, known as the enablement requirement, is satisfied when the specification describes the claimed invention in such detail that one of skill in the art would be able to make and use the claimed invention without undue experimentation. *Nat'l Recovery Techs., Inc. v. Magnetic Separation Sys., Inc.*, 166 F.3d 1190, 1195–96 (Fed. Cir. 1999). It is well settled, however, that enablement does not require the disclosure of routine details that are known to those of skill in the art. *Hybritech Inc.* v. *Monoclonal Antibodies, Inc.*, 802 F.2d 1367, 1384 (Fed. Cir. 1986) ("[A] patent need not teach, and preferably omits, what is well known in the art."). In determining whether an inventor has complied with the enablement requirement, the jury may consider such evidence as:

> (1) the quantity of experimentation necessary, (2) the amount of direction or guidance presented, (3) the presence or absence of working examples, (4) the nature of the invention, (5) the state of the prior art, (6) the relative skill of those in the art, (7) the predictability or unpredictability of the art, and (8) the breadth of the claims.

Enzo Biochem, Inc. v. *Calgene, Inc.*, 188 F.3d 1362, 1371 (Fed. Cir. 1999) (quoting *In re Wands*, 858 F.2d 731, 737 (Fed. Cir. 1988)).

The third requirement, known as the best mode requirement, is satisfied when an inventor discloses the best mode of practicing the claimed invention known to him or her at the time the patent application was filed. In making this determination, the jury must undertake two factual inquiries. First, did the inventor know of a best mode of practicing the claimed invention at the time the patent application was filed and, if so, was that best mode disclosed in the specification in sufficient detail to enable one of skill in the art to practice it without undue experimentation. *See Mentor H/S, Inc.* v. *Med. Device Alliance, Inc.*, 244 F.3d 1365, 1375 (Fed. Cir. 2001); *N. Telecom Ltd.* v. *Samsung Elecs. Co.*, 215 F.3d 1281, 1289 (Fed. Cir. 2000).

35 U.S.C. § 112, ¶ 2

35 U.S.C. § 112, ¶ 2 (1984) provides:

> The specification shall conclude with one or more claims particularly pointing out and distinctly claiming the subject matter which the applicant regards at his invention.

This section sets out a requirement for definite patent claims. Claims that are indefinite, that is, claims that do not set forth the invention in a sufficiently clear manner, are invalid.

The requirement for definite claims is satisfied when the patent claims are drafted in a manner that provides notice to one of skill in the art of the metes and bounds of the claimed invention. *Personalized Media Communications* v. *Int'l Trade Comm'n*, 161 F.3d 696, 705 (Fed. Cir. 1998). The inquiry of whether or not a skilled person would understand these metes and bounds is "typically limited to the way one of skill in the art would interpret the claims in view of the written description portion of the specification." *Solomon* v. *Kimberly-Clark Corp.*, 216 F.3d 1372, 1378–79 (Fed. Cir. 2000).

9.1.1 Written Description

A patent must contain a written description of the [product or process] claimed in the patent. In order to satisfy the written description requirement, the patent specification must describe each and every limitation of a patent claim, although the exact words found in the claim need not be used.

[Defendant] contends that claims _____ of the _____ patent are invalid for lack of an adequate written description of the claimed invention. If you find that [defendant] has proved that it is highly probable that the _____ patent does not contain a written description of the invention covered by any of these claims, then you must find that the claim is invalid.

NOTE

The written description requirement of 35 U.S.C. § 112, ¶ 1 requires that a patent specification contain a description of every claim limitation. *Lockwood* v. *Am. Airlines, Inc.*, 107 F.3d 1565, 1572 (Fed. Cir. 1997). The question of whether or not patent claims must include every element disclosed in the specification in order to satisfy the written description requirement was considered in *Gentry Gallery, Inc.* v. *Berkline Corp.*, 134 F.3d 1473 (Fed. Cir. 1998). In that case, the patent disclosed a sectional sofa with a pair of reclining seats, and a console containing the controls between the reclining seats. The patent claims, however, did not specify the location of the controls for the recliner on the console. The Court found that the claims omitted an "essential element" of the invention and therefore did not meet the written description requirement of § 112, ¶ 1.

For a period, courts were uncertain whether *Gentry Gallery* created a new "essential element" test under § 112, ¶ 1. *See, e.g., Reiffin* v. *Microsoft Corp.*, 214 F.3d 1342, 1348 (Fed. Cir. 2000) (Newman, J., concurring); *Purdue Pharma, L.P.* v. *F.H. Faulding & Co.*, 48 F. Supp. 2d 420, 431 (D. Del. 1999), *aff'd*, 230 F.3d 1320 (Fed. Cir. 2000). However, in *Cooper Cameron Corp.* v. *Kvaerner Oilfield Prod.*, 291 F.3d 1317, 1323 (Fed. Cir. 2002), a panel of the Federal Circuit explained that its analysis in *Gentry Gallery* did not create a new "essential element" test. Rather, *Gentry* "merely expounded upon the unremarkable proposition that a broad claim is invalid when the entirety of the specification clearly indicates that the invention is of a much narrower scope." *Id*.

AUTHORITIES

PIN/NIP, Inc. v. *Platte Chem. Co.*, 304 F.3d 1235 (Fed. Cir. 2002); *Enzo Biochem, Inc.* v. *Gen-Probe, Inc.*, 285 F.3d 1013, 1018 (Fed. Cir. 2002); *Turbocare Div. of Demag Delaval Turbomachinery Corp.* v. *General Elect. Co.*, 264 F.3d 1111, 1118 (Fed. Cir. 2001); *Purdue Pharma L.P.* v. *Faulding, Inc.*, 230 F.3d 1320, 1323 (Fed. Cir. 2000); *Lampi Corp.* v. *Am. Power Prods., Inc.*, 228 F.3d 1365, 1377–78 (Fed. Cir. 2000); *Reiffin* v. *Microsoft Corp.*, 214 F.3d 1342, 1345–46 (Fed. Cir. 2000); *Union Oil Co. of Cal.* v. *Atl. Richfield Co.*, 208 F.3d 989, 996–1001 (Fed. Cir. 2000); *Sun Tiger Inc.* v. *Scientific Research Funding Group*, 189 F.3d 1327, 1334 (Fed. Cir. 1999); *Tronzo* v. *Biomet Inc.*, 156 F.3d 1154, 1158–60 (Fed. Cir. 1998); *Gentry Gallery, Inc.* v. *Berkline Corp.*, 134 F.3d 1473, 1478–80 (Fed. Cir. 1998); *Lockwood* v. *Am. Airlines, Inc.*, 107 F.3d 1565, 1572 (Fed. Cir. 1997).

9.1.2   Enablement

The written description of the invention claimed in a patent must contain enough detail to teach, or enable, persons skilled in the field of the invention to make and use the invention. This is referred to as the enablement requirement. If the patent does not enable a skilled person to practice the [product or process] of a patent claim, then the claim is invalid.

In considering whether or not the written description of a patent meets the enablement requirement, you must keep in mind that patents are written for persons of skill in the field of the invention. Thus, a patent need not expressly state information that skilled persons would be likely to know or could obtain.

The fact that some experimentation may be required for a skilled person to practice the claimed invention does not mean that a patent's written description does not meet the enablement requirement. A written description is enabling so long as undue experimentation is not needed to make or use the invention. A permissible amount of experimentation is that amount that is appropriate for the complexity of the field of the invention and for the level of expertise and knowledge of persons skilled in that field.

[Defendant] contends that claims _____ of the _____ patent are invalid for lack of enablement. If you find that [defendant] has proved that it is highly probable that the written description of the _____ patent does not enable a skilled person to make and use a [product or process] covered by any of these claims without undue experimentation, then you must find that the claim is invalid.

NOTE

"The enablement requirement of § 112 demands that the patent specification enable 'those skilled in the art to make and use the full scope of the claimed invention without undue experimentation.'" *Nat'l Recovery Techs., Inc.* v. *Magnetic Sep-*

aration Sys., Inc., 166 F.3d 1190, 1195–96 (Fed. Cir. 1999) (citations omitted). Thus, in order to satisfy the enablement requirement, an inventor's disclosure must be commensurate with the scope of the claimed invention. *Id.* ("The enablement requirement ensures that the public knowledge is enriched by the patent specification to a degree at least commensurate with the scope of the claims.") The disclosure of a single embodiment or species may not adequately enable a claim directed to a genus or to a number of embodiments or species. *E.g., Enzo Biochem, Inc.* v. *Calgene, Inc.*, 188 F.3d 1362, 1371 (Fed. Cir. 1999) (claims directed to the use of genetic "antisense" technology to regulate gene expression in both bacterial and non-bacterial cells are not enabled by the patent specification, which discloses the use of the technology in only one type of bacterial cell).

AUTHORITIES

Durel Corp. v. *Osram Sylvania, Inc.*, 256 F.3d 1298, 1306 (2001); *Union Pac. Resources Co.* v. *Chesapeake Energy Corp.*, 236 F.3d 684, 690–92 (Fed. Cir. 2001); *Ajinomoto Co.* v. *Archer-Daniels-Midland Co.*, 228 F.3d 1338, 1345–46 (Fed. Cir. 2000); *Enzo Biochem, Inc.* v. *Calgene, Inc.*, 188 F.3d 1362, 1369–78 (Fed. Cir. 1999); *Nat'l Recovery Techs., Inc.* v. *Magnetic Separation Sys., Inc.*, 166 F.3d 1190, 1195–98 (Fed. Cir. 1999).

9.1.3   Best Mode

The patent laws require that if the inventor knew of a best way, or "mode," of making and using the claimed invention at the time the application for the patent was filed, then the patent specification must contain a description of that mode. This is called the "best mode" requirement.

The purpose of the best mode requirement is to ensure that the public obtains a full disclosure of how to carry out the invention claimed in the patent. It prevents an inventor from obtaining a patent, while at the same time not disclosing to the public his or her preferred way of making or using the claimed invention. The inventor must disclose the best mode he or she knew of for carrying out the invention as it is described in the patent claims.

Determining whether or not an inventor disclosed his or her best mode involves answering two questions. The first question relates to what the inventor knew at the time the application for the patent was filed. In this case, that date is _____. The first question is: At the time the application was filed, did the inventor know of a way, or mode, of making or using the invention claimed in the patent that the inventor considered to be better than any other mode? This first question is subjective; that is, it involves only what the inventor thought or believed.

If you find that the answer to the first question is no—that is, the inventor did not know of a best mode of making or using his or her invention at the time the application was filed—you should stop there. The patent cannot be invalid for failure to disclose the best mode if the inventor did not know of a best mode when the application was filed.

If you find that the inventor did know of a best mode at the time the application was filed, then you must consider the second question, which is: Does the patent contain a description of the inventor's best mode that is sufficient to enable a person skilled in the art to carry out the best mode? This question is objective. It depends, not on what the inventor thought or understood, but rather on what a person skilled in the field of the invention reading the patent would understand.

A patent describes the best mode if it contains enough information that a skilled person reading the patent would be able to carry out the best mode without undue experimentation. That means that a skilled person reading the patent would be able to make and use the best mode of the invention using only an amount of experimentation that is appropriate for the complexity of the field of the invention and for the level of expertise and knowledge of persons skilled in that field.

[Defendant] contends that claims _____ of the _____ patent are invalid for failure to disclose the best mode. If you find that the [defendant] has proved that it is highly probable that (1) the inventor on the _____ patent had a best mode of practicing the invention claimed in claims _____ of the _____ patent at the time the application was filed, and (2) the _____ patent does not contain a written description that would enable a skilled person to make and use that best mode without undue experimentation, then you must find that these claims are invalid.

NOTE

Because the duty to disclose the best mode of practicing a claimed invention applies only to modes actually contemplated by the inventor at the time the application was filed, the best mode analysis is necessarily a two-step inquiry. First, the jury must determine whether or not the inventor contemplated a best mode of practicing the claimed invention at the time the application was filed. If the inventor had contemplated such a best mode, then the jury must determine whether or not the patent contains an enabling disclosure of the best mode.

Thus, the instruction tells the jury that it need go no further if it finds that the answer to the first question is no. If there is a dispute about whether or not the inventor had in fact contemplated a particular "best" mode as of the patent's filing date, consideration should be given to having the jury decide the second question, even if the jury finds that the inventor was unaware of the alleged best mode as of the patent's filing date. This will preclude the need for a remand if the jury's finding that the inventor had not contemplated a best mode is overturned on appeal.

In recent decisions, the Federal Circuit emphasized that a patent owner's duty under the best mode requirement of 35 U.S.C. § 112, ¶ 1 is limited by the claimed subject matter. *See Mentor H/S, Inc.* v. *Med. Device Alliance, Inc.*, 244 F.3d 1365, 1375 (Fed. Cir. 2001); *Bayer AG* v. *Schein Pharma.*, 301 F.3d 1306, 1314–1320 (Fed. Cir. 2002). Thus, a patent owner is under no duty to disclose preferred modes that fall outside the scope of the claims. As stated by the Court in *Mentor*, "[a]n applicant is only obliged to disclose unclaimed elements when they are necessary to the operation of the invention." *Mentor*, 244 F.3d at 1375.

AUTHORITIES

Bayer AG v. *Schein Pharma., Inc.*, 301 F.3d 1306, 1314–1320 (Fed. Cir. 2002); *Mentor H/S, Inc.* v. *Med. Device Alliance, Inc.*, 244 F.3d 1365 (Fed. Cir. 2001); *Eli Lilly & Co.* v. *Barr Labs., Inc.*, 222 F.3d 973, 980–84 (Fed. Cir. 2000); *N. Telecom Ltd.* v. *Samsung Elecs. Co.*, 215 F.3d 1281, 1285–89 (Fed. Cir. 2000); *United States Gypsum Co.* v. *Nat'l Gypsum Co.*, 74 F.3d 1209, 1212 (Fed. Cir. 1996); *Glaxo Inc.* v. *Novopharm Ltd.*, 52 F.3d 1043, 1049–52 (Fed. Cir. 1995).

9.1.4 Definiteness

The patent laws have requirements for the way in which patent claims are written. Patent claims must be sufficiently clear that a person of ordinary skill in the field of the invention reading them is able to determine what the claims cover and what they do not cover. A person of ordinary skill is a person of average education and training in the field. If a patent claim does not meet this requirement, then the claim is said to be indefinite, and the claim is invalid.

The amount of detail required for a claim to be definite depends on the particular invention, the prior art and the description of the invention contained in the patent. A patent claim, when read along with the rest of the patent, must reasonably inform those skilled in the field of the invention what the patent claims cover. Simply because claim language may not be precise does not automatically mean that the claim is indefinite. The claim language need only be as precise as the subject matter permits.

[Defendant] contends that claims _____ of the _____ patent are invalid because the language of the claims is indefinite. [[Defendant] contends that claims _____ of the _____ patent are indefinite because they use the word "about" to modify the claim term _____. The use of the word "about," or similar language, does not by itself cause the claim to be indefinite. In order to decide whether or not the use of the word "about" in claims _____ renders those claims indefinite, you must consider whether or not the _____ patent provides some guidance about what is included within the claim term "about _____." You must also consider whether or not a person of ordinary skill in the field reading the patent would understand what is included within the claim term.]

If you find that [defendant] has proved that it is highly probable that claims _____ of the _____ patent are indefinite because a person of ordinary skill in the art would not understand what is, and what is not, covered by the claims, you must then find that those claims are invalid.

NOTE

In determining whether a claim complies with the definiteness requirement of 35 U.S.C. § 112, ¶ 2, the focus is on whether one skilled in the art would understand the metes and bounds of the claimed invention when read in light of the specification. *LNP Eng'g Plastics, Inc.* v. *Miller Waste Mills, Inc.*, 275 F.3d 1347, 1357 (Fed. Cir. 2001); *Union Pac. Resources Co.* v. *Chesapeake Energy Corp.*, 236 F.3d 684, 692 (Fed. Cir. 2001). The Federal Circuit has noted that this inquiry is a matter of claim construction. However, unlike other issues related to claim construction, the claims are presumed to comply with § 112 ¶ 2. *S3 Inc.* v. *nVIDIA Corp.*, 259 F.3d 1364, 1367 (Fed. Cir. 2001) ("The claims as granted are accompanied by a presumption of validity based on compliance with, *inter alia*, § 112, ¶ 2."); *Budde* v. *Harley-Davidson, Inc.*, 250 F.3d 1369, 1376 (Fed. Cir. 2001).

The Federal Circuit has long recognized that certain claim terms, such as "about," "substantially" and "approximately" are by definition imprecise. This imprecision, however, does not render the claim per se indefinite. Rather, the court must construe these types of claim terms in light of the patent specification and prosecution history. *Pall Corp.* v. *Micron Separations, Inc.*, 66 F.3d 1217 (Fed. Cir. 1995); *Eiselstein* v. *Frank*, 52 F.3d 1035, 1040–41 (Fed. Cir. 1995); *W.L. Gore & Assoc., Inc.* v. *Garlock, Inc.*, 842 F.2d 1275, 1280 (Fed. Cir. 1988); *Uniroyal, Inc.* v. *Rudkin-Wiley Corp.*, 837 F.2d 1044, 1056 (Fed. Cir. 1988).

After construing the claim term in light of the patent specification and prosecution history, if one skilled in the art still cannot determine the scope of the claims, the court should then find that the claim is invalid for being indefinite. *Union Pac.*, 236 F.3d at 692 (holding that the claim term "comparing" was susceptible to two different constructions and was, therefore, invalid for being indefinite).

AUTHORITIES

Creo Prod. v. *Presstek, Inc.*, 305 F.3d 1337 (Fed. Cir. 2002); *LNP Eng'g Plastics, Inc.* v. *Miller Waste Mills, Inc.*, 275 F.3d 1347,

1357 (Fed. Cir. 2001); *S3 Inc.* v. *nVIDIA Corp.*, 259 F.3d 1364, 1367 (Fed. Cir. 2001); *Budde* v. *Harley-Davidson, Inc.*, 250 F.3d 1369, 1376 (Fed. Cir. 2001); *Union Pac. Resources Co.* v. *Chesapeake Energy Corp.*, 236 F.3d 684, 692 (Fed. Cir. 2001); *Solomon* v. *Kimberly-Clark Corp.*, 216 F.3d 1372, 1378–80 (Fed. Cir. 2000); *Atmel Corp.* v. *Info. Storage Devices, Inc.*, 198 F.3d 1374, 1378–82 (Fed. Cir. 1999); *Personalized Media Communications, L.L.C.* v. *Int'l Trade Comm'n*, 161 F.3d 696, 700 n.5, 705 (Fed. Cir. 1998); *In re Dossel*, 115 F.3d 942 (Fed. Cir. 1997); *Pall Corp.* v. *Micron Separations, Inc.*, 66 F.3d 1211, 1217 (Fed. Cir. 1995); *Eiselstein* v. *Frank*, 52 F.3d 1035, 1040–41 (Fed. Cir. 1995); *In re Donaldson Co.*, 16 F.3d 1189 (Fed. Cir. 1994); *N. Am. Vaccine, Inc.* v. *Am. Cynamid Co.*, 7 F.3d 1571, 1579–80 (Fed. Cir. 1993); *W.L. Gore & Assoc., Inc.* v. *Garlock, Inc.*, 842 F.2d 1275, 1280 (Fed. Cir. 1988); *Uniroyal, Inc.* v. *Rudkin-Wiley Corp.*, 837 F.2d 1044, 1056 (Fed. Cir. 1988).

9.2 Prior Art—Introduction

A fundamental tenet of patent law is that "no patent should be granted which withdraws from the public domain technology already available to the public." *Kimberly-Clark Corp.* v. *Johnson & Johnson*, 745 F.2d 1437, 1453 (Fed. Cir. 1984). The prior art includes that which is present, either expressly or inherently, in a particular item of prior art. *Acromed Corp.* v. *Sofamor Danek Group, Inc.*, 253 F.3d 1371, 1379 (Fed. Cir. 2001). Prior art will invalidate a patent claim if each and every limitation of the claim is disclosed in a single item of prior art (anticipation under 35 U.S.C. § 102), or if it would have been obvious to a person of ordinary skill in the art to combine what was known at the time the claimed invention was made to come up with the invention (obviousness under 35 U.S.C. § 103).

The Federal Circuit has defined the prior art to be the "knowledge that is available, including what would be obvious from it, at a given time, to a person of ordinary skill in an art." *Kimberly-Clark*, 745 F.2d at 1453. 35 U.S.C. § 102 (1984 & Supp. 2001) sets out the various categories of prior art recognized under the patent laws:

A person shall be entitled to a patent unless—

(a) the invention was known or used by others in this country, or patented or described in a printed publication in this or a foreign country, before the invention thereof by the applicant for patent, or

(b) the invention was patented or described in a printed publication in this or a foreign country or in public use or on sale in this country, more than one year prior to the date of the application for patent in the United States, or

* * * *

(e) The invention was described in—

(1) an application for patent, published under section 122(b), by another filed in the United States before the invention by the applicant for patent, except that an

international application filed under the treaty defined in section 351(a) shall have the effect under this subsection of a national application published under section 122(b) only if the international application designating the United States was published under Article 21(2)(a) of such treaty in the English language; or

(2) a patent granted on an application for patent by another filed in the United States before the invention by the applicant for patent, except that a patent shall not be deemed filed in the United States for the purposes of this subsection based on the filing of an international application, filed under the treaty defined in section 351(a); or

(f) he did not himself invent the subject matter sought to be patented, or

(g) (1) during the course of an interference conducted under section 135 or section 291, another inventor involved therein establishes, to the extent permitted in section 104, that before such person's invention thereof the invention was made by such other inventor and not abandoned, suppressed, or concealed, or (2) before such person's invention thereof, the invention was made in this country by another inventor who had not abandoned, suppressed, or concealed it. In determining priority of invention under this subsection, there shall be considered not only the respective dates of conception and reduction to practice of the invention, but also the reasonable diligence of one who was first to conceive and last to reduce to practice, from a time prior to conception by the other.

Items of prior art falling within these categories may be relied upon individually for anticipation of a claimed invention, or combined for obviousness.

If the prior art status of an item of prior art is uncontested, then the prior art may be identified to the jury without instruction as to the legal requirements for the categories into which the items of prior art fall. If the prior art status is contested, then Instructions 9.3.1–9.3.10 may be read to the jury, as applicable, for the disputed categories of prior art.

9.3 The Prior Art

Under the patent laws, a person is entitled to a patent only if the invention claimed in the patent is new and unobvious in light of what came before. That which came before is referred to as the "prior art."

[Defendant] is relying on various items of prior art. [Defendant] and [plaintiff] agree that the following items are prior art, and there is no dispute that these items came before the invention claimed in the _____ patent:

[List uncontested prior art]

[Defendant] is also relying on items that [plaintiff] does not agree are prior art. [Defendant] must prove by the highly probable standard that these items are prior art. In order to do so, [defendant] must prove that the items fall within one or more of the different categories of prior art recognized by the patent laws. These categories include **[list only categories that apply to the items of contested prior art]**:

First, anything that was publicly known or used in the United States by someone other than the inventor before the inventor made the invention.

Second, anything that was in public use or on sale in the United States more than one year before the application for the patent was filed.

Third, anything that was patented or described in a printed publication anywhere in the world before the inventor made the invention, or more than one year before the application for the patent was filed.

Fourth, anything that was invented by another person [in this country] before the inventor made the invention, if the other person did not abandon, suppress or conceal his or her prior invention.

Fifth, anything that was described in a patent that issued from a patent application filed in the United States or certain foreign countries before the inventor made the invention.

NOTE

Section 102(g)(1) (Supp. 2001) provides for reliance on activities in NAFTA or WTO countries if those activities were successfully relied on to prove priority of invention in an interference. If this applies to your case, omit the words "in this country," otherwise include them.

9.3.1 Prior Art—Date of Invention

Many of the different categories of prior art refer to the date at which the inventor made the invention. This is called the "date of invention."

[If the date of invention is not in dispute]:

In this case the date of invention is _____.

[If the date of invention is in dispute]:

I will now explain to you how to determine this date.

There are two parts to the making of an invention. The inventor has the idea of the invention. This is referred to as "conception" of the invention. A conception of an invention is complete when the inventor has formed the idea of how to make and use every aspect of the claimed invention, and all that is required is that it be made without the need for any further inventive effort. The actual making of the invention is referred to as "reduction to practice." An invention is said to be "reduced to practice" when it is made and shown to work for its intended purpose.

[Include the following only to the extent it is relevant to issues in the case]:

Under the patent laws, the date of invention is generally the date that the patent application was filed. This is also referred to as a "constructive reduction to practice." In this case, that date is _____. Ordinarily, art that came before the application's filing date is prior art to the patent claims.

There are, however, two circumstances under which art dated before the application filing date is not prior art. The first occurs when the inventor on the patent reduced the invention to practice before the date of the art. In this case, the art is not prior art to the _____ patent.

The second circumstance under which art dated before the application filing date is not prior art occurs when the inventor conceived of the invention before the date of the art and exercised reasonable diligence from just before the date of the art up to the date of the inventor's reduction to practice. In that case, the art is not prior art to the _____ patent.

Remember, reduction to practice occurs either as of the filing of the patent application or when the invention was actually made and was shown to work for its intended purpose. Reasonable diligence means that the inventor worked continuously on reducing the invention to practice. Interruptions necessitated by the everyday problems and obligations of the inventor or others working with him or her do not prevent a finding of diligence.

I will now describe the specific requirements for the prior art categories relied on by [defendant] in this case.

NOTE

Under the Patent Act, an invention consists of two parts, the mental part of the invention, known as the conception, and the physical part of the invention, known as the reduction to practice.

Conception is "'the formation in the mind of the inventor, of a definite and permanent idea of the complete and operative invention.'" *Burroughs Wellcome Co.* v. *Barr Labs.*, 40 F.3d 1223, 1228 (Fed. Cir. 1994) (citation omitted). "Conception is complete only when the idea is so clearly defined in the inventor's mind that only ordinary skill would be necessary to reduce the invention to practice, without extensive research or experimentation." *Id*.

Such acts as (1) posing a problem or (2) setting forth a general goal or research plan, have been found not to constitute a conception. *Burroughs Wellcome Co.* v. *Barr Labs., Inc.*, 40 F.3d 1223, 1228 (Fed. Cir. 1994); *Morgan* v. *Hirsch*, 728 F.2d 1449, 1452 (Fed. Cir. 1984). In addition, because conception is the mental part of the invention, an inventor's testimony, standing alone, is insufficient to prove conception. *Mahurkar* v. *C.R. Bard*, 79 F.3d 1572, 1577 (Fed. Cir. 1996) ("This requirement arose out of a concern that inventors testifying in patent infringement cases would be tempted to remember facts favorable to their case by the lure of protecting their patent or defeating another's patent."). Courts, therefore, require "corroborating evidence of a contemporaneous disclosure that would enable one skilled in the art to make the invention." *Burroughs*, 40 F.3d at 1227–28.

In assessing corroboration of oral testimony, courts apply a "rule of reason" analysis. *Mahurkar v. C.R. Bard*, 79 F.3d 1572, 1577 (Fed. Cir. 1996). "Under a rule of reason analysis, 'an evaluation of all pertinent evidence must be made so that a sound determination of credibility of the inventor's story may be reached.'" *Id.* (citation omitted).

Reducing the claimed invention to practice is the second part to an invention. Thus, an inventor's date of invention is at least as early as the date the invention was reduced to practice. Reduction to practice may be accomplished in two ways. One way is to make a physical embodiment that includes all of the limitations of the claimed invention. This is known as an "actual" reduction to practice. A second way is to file a patent application disclosing the invention. This is known as a "constructive" reduction to practice.

If the date of invention for a claimed invention is uncontested, then the invention date may be provided to the jury without instruction as to the legal requirements for establishing a date of invention. If the invention date is contested, then this instruction should be read to the jury.

AUTHORITIES

Mycogen Plant Sci., Inc. v. *Monsanto Co.*, 243 F.3d 1316, 1330 (Fed. Cir. 2001); *Singh* v. *Brake*, 222 F.3d 1362, 1366–70 (Fed. Cir. 2000); *Genentech Inc.* v. *Chiron Corp.*, 220 F.3d 1345, 1351 (Fed. Cir. 2000); *Bruning* v. *Hirose*, 161 F.3d 681, 684–85 (Fed. Cir. 1998); *Cooper* v. *Goldfarb*, 154 F.3d 1321, 1326–31 (Fed. Cir. 1998); *Hyatt* v. *Boone*, 146 F.3d 1348, 1352–55 (Fed. Cir. 1998); *Estee Lauder Inc.* v. *L'Oreal, S.A.*, 129 F.3d 588, 592–93 (Fed. Cir. 1997); *Mahurkar* v. *C.R. Bard, Inc.*, 79 F.3d 1572, 1577–79 (Fed. Cir. 1996); *Burroughs Wellcome Co.* v. *Barr Labs.*, 40 F.3d 1223, 1228 (Fed. Cir. 1994); *Griffith* v. *Kanamaru*, 816 F.2d 624,

626 (Fed. Cir. 1987); *Bey* v. *Kollonitsch*, 806 F.2d 1024, 1026 (Fed. Cir. 1986); *Morgan* v. *Hirsch*, 728 F.2d 1449, 1452 (Fed. Cir. 1984).

9.3.2   Prior Public Knowledge or Use—in General

Instructions 9.3.3–9.3.5 relate to prior art falling within 35 U.S.C. § 102(a) and 35 U.S.C. § 102(b)—prior public use or knowledge of a claimed invention (or of a product or process that renders a claimed invention obvious). Instruction 9.3.3 describes the legal requirements for prior art under 35 U.S.C. § 102(a). That category relates to prior public knowledge or use by persons other than the inventor in the United States before the date of invention for the claimed invention. Instruction 9.3.4 describes the requirements for prior art under 35 U.S.C. § 102(b). Such prior art constitutes a prior use of the claimed invention more than one year before the filing date of a patent application.

Instruction 9.3.3 should be used when only prior knowledge or use under § 102(a) is at issue in the case, but not prior public use under 35 U.S.C. § 102(b). Similarly, Instruction 9.3.4 should be used when only prior public use under § 102(b) is at issue, but not prior knowledge under 35 U.S.C. § 102(a). If both are at issue, Instruction 9.3.5, which explains the differences between the legal requirements for the two different prior art categories, should be used.

9.3.3 Prior Art—Prior Knowledge or Use by Another in the United States

Knowledge or use in the United States of a patented invention can be prior art to the patent claims. The knowledge or use will be prior art if it meets the following requirements:

First, the knowledge or use must be by someone other than the inventor.

Second, the knowledge or use must be before the inventor's date of invention.

Third, the knowledge or use must be in the United States. Prior knowledge or use outside the United States cannot be relied upon to invalidate a patent claim.

Fourth, the knowledge or use must have been public. Private or secret knowledge or use by someone other than the inventor is not prior art.

In this case, [defendant] relies on _____ as a prior public knowledge or use before the date of invention of the _____ patent.

NOTE

Use this instruction only when prior public knowledge or use under 35 U.S.C. § 102(a) is at issue in the case, but not prior public use under 35 U.S.C. § 102(b).

AUTHORITIES

Woodland Trust v. *Flowertree Nursery, Inc.*, 148 F.3d 1368, 1370 (Fed. Cir. 1998); *Lockwood* v. *Am. Airlines, Inc.*, 107 F.3d 1565, 1570 (Fed. Cir. 1997); *Lamb-Weston, Inc.* v. *McCain Foods, Ltd.*, 78 F.3d 540, 544 (Fed. Cir. 1996).

9.3.4 Prior Art—Public Use More Than One Year before the Application Was Filed

The use of a product or process of a patent claim more than one year before the filing date of the application for the patent may be prior art to the patent claim.

First, the use must occur more than one year before the patent application was filed. In this case, that date is _____. The date of invention for the patent claims is irrelevant to this category of prior art. If the public use is more than one year before the patent application was filed, then that public use may be prior art, regardless of the date of invention.

Second, the use may be by anyone, including the inventor or patent owner.

Third, if the use was by someone other than the inventor, the use must have been public in order to be prior art.

Fourth, a use more than one year before the application filing date by the inventor or the patent owner will be prior art if it was for commercial purposes, even if done in secret.

In this case, [defendant] relies on _____ as a public use more than one year before the filing date of the application for the _____ patent.

NOTE

Use this instruction only when prior public use under 35 U.S.C. § 102(b) is at issue, but not prior knowledge or use under 35 U.S.C. § 102(a).

AUTHORITIES

Mitsubishi Elec. Corp. v. *Ampex Corp.*, 190 F. 3d 1300, 1303–05 (Fed. Cir. 1999); *Woodland Trust* v. *Flowertree Nursery, Inc.*, 148 F.3d 1368, 1370 (Fed. Cir. 1998); *Evans Cooling Sys., Inc.* v. *Gen. Motors Corp.*, 125 F.3d 1448, 1452–54 (Fed. Cir. 1997); *Lough* v. *Brunswick Corp.*, 86 F.3d 1113, 1119 (Fed. Cir. 1996), *reh'g en banc denied*, 103 F.3d 1517 (Fed. Cir. 1997); *Baxter Int'l, Inc.* v. *Cobe Labs., Inc.*, 88 F.3d 1054, 1058–60 (Fed. Cir. 1996).

9.3.5   Prior Art—Prior Public Use or Knowledge

The prior public use of a claimed invention may be prior art to the patent claims under two different circumstances. The first is where the invention was publicly known or used by someone other than the inventor before the date of invention by the inventor on the patent. The second is where the inventor, the patent owner, or anyone else publicly used the invention more than one year before the application for the patent was filed.

In both circumstances, the public use must have been in the United States. Prior public use or knowledge of the claimed invention outside the United States is not prior art to a patent claim.

Use or knowledge by someone other than the inventor may be prior art if it was before the date of invention by the inventor on the patent, or more than one year before the filing of the application for the patent. In either case, a prior use by someone other than the inventor or the patent owner will not be prior art unless it was public. Private or secret knowledge or use by another is not prior art.

If the prior use was more than one year before the filing date of the application for the patent, then the date of invention for the patent claims is irrelevant. A public use more than one year before the patent application was filed will be prior art regardless of the date of invention.

A prior use more than one year before the application filing date by the inventor or the patent owner will be prior art if it was for commercial purposes, even if it was done in secret.

In this case, [defendant] relies on _____ as a prior public use or knowledge before the inventor's date of invention, and [defendant] relies on _____ as a prior public use more than one year before the filing date of the application for the _____ patent.

NOTE

Use this instruction instead of instructions 9.3.3 and 9.3.4 when both prior knowledge or use under 35 U.S.C. § 102(a) and § 102(b) are at issue in the case.

AUTHORITIES

Woodland Trust v. *Flowertree Nursery, Inc.*, 148 F.3d 1368, 1370 (Fed. Cir. 1998); *Lockwood* v. *Am. Airlines, Inc.*, 107 F.3d 1565, 1570 (Fed. Cir. 1997).

9.3.6 Prior Art—On-Sale or Offered for Sale More Than One Year before the Application Was Filed

The sale or offer for sale in the United States of a product may be prior art to a patent claim covering the product or a method of making the product if the product was sold or offered for sale more than one year before the application for the patent was filed. In this case, that date is _____. The date of invention for the patent claims is irrelevant to this category of prior art. If the sale or offer for sale of a product is more than one year before the patent application was filed, then the product or method of making it may be prior art, regardless of the date of invention.

[If the sale or offer for sale was of a patented product, then it may be prior art regardless of who made the offer.]

[If the sale or offer for sale was of a product made by a patented process, and if the sale or offer for sale is by the inventor, the patent owner, or a representative of the inventor or patent owner, then the process may be prior art to the patent claims, even if it was done in secret. This is because the law considers it unfair for a patent owner to get a commercial benefit from the invention while waiting more than one year before filing a patent application.]

[If the sale or offer for sale of a product made by a patented process was by someone other than the inventor, the patent owner, or a representative of the inventor or patent owner, then the sale or offer for sale of the product may make the process prior art only if the process was public. Secret use of a process by another person is not prior art, even if the product made by the process is sold.]

In order for there to be an offer for sale, two requirements must be met. First, the product must have been the subject of a commercial offer for sale. Second, the product must be "ready for patenting."

Even a single offer for sale to a single customer may be a commercial offer, even if the customer does not accept the offer.

An invention is ready for patenting if the product offered for sale has been developed to the point where there was reason to expect that it would work for its intended purpose. The product may be ready for patenting even if it is not ready for commercial production, or has not been technically perfected.

In this case, [defendant] relies on _____ as a [sale/offer for sale] more than one year before the filing date of the application for the _____ patent.

NOTE

This instruction relates to the "on sale" prior art category of 35 U.S.C. § 102(b). In order for a product or process used to make a product to be prior art under this category, the product must have been sold or offered for sale more than one year before the patent application claiming that product or process was filed. Under this category, no distinction is made between an inventor or a third party who has sold or offered for sale a patented product prior to the critical date. Either party's actions are considered prior art to the patent.

A distinction is made, however, between an inventor or a third party who has sold or offered for sale a product that was made by a patented process prior to the critical date. In the first instance, the inventor's secret use of the patented process is deemed to be prior art. *See D.L. Auld Co.* v. *Chroma Graphics Corp.*, 714 F.2d 1144, 1147 (Fed. Cir. 1983) (holding that the inventor's secret use of the patented process rendered the claims invalid under 35 U.S.C. § 102(b)). In contrast, the third party's secret use is not considered to be prior art to the patent. *See W.L. Gore & Assocs., Inc.* v. *Garlock, Inc.*, 721 F.2d 1540, 1548–50 (Fed. Cir. 1983) (holding that a third party's secret use of the patented process did not render the claims invalid under § 102(b)). The Court in *W.L. Gore* explained that:

> As between a prior inventor who benefits from a process by selling its product but suppresses, conceals, or otherwise keeps the process from the public, and a later inventor who promptly files a patent application from which the public will gain a disclosure of the process, the law favors the latter.

W.L. Gore, 721 F.2d at 1550.

The issue of when a product has been offered for sale was addressed by the Supreme Court in *Pfaff* v. *Wells Elecs., Inc.*, 525 U.S. 55 (1998). In that case, the Supreme Court considered how far along in its development an invention must be in order for it to be the subject of an offer for sale. The Court rejected the test in the case law requiring that an invention be "substantially complete" before it may be "on sale" for purposes of 35 U.S.C. § 102(b), reasoning that such a rule "seriously undermines the interest of certainty." *Id.* at 65–66. Instead, the Court held that an invention may be offered for sale if it was "ready for patenting" at the time of the offer.

The Court held that an invention is ready for patenting if, at the time of the offer, the invention was reduced to practice or the inventor had prepared drawings or other descriptions of the invention that were sufficiently detailed to enable a skilled person to practice the invention. *Id.* at 67–68; *see also Robotic Vision Sys., Inc.* v. *View Eng'g, Inc.*, 249 F.3d 1307 (Fed. Cir. 2001) (holding that the invention was ready for patenting because the inventor's disclosure enabled a co-worker to practice the claimed invention). In other words, for an invention to be ready for patenting, the inventor must be able to "provide an enabling disclosure as required by 35 U.S.C. § 112." *Space Sys./Loral, Inc.* v. *Lockheed Martin Corp.*, 271 F.3d 1076, 1080 (Fed. Cir. 2001).

The Federal Circuit has also made clear that general contract principles should be applied when determining whether an offer for sale has been made. *See Group One, Ltd.* v. *Hallmark Cards, Inc.*, 254 F.3d 1041, 1046–47 (Fed. Cir. 2001) (holding that an offer "must meet the level of an offer for sale in the contract sense, one that would be understood as such in the commercial community"); *Scaltech, Inc.* v. *Retech/Tetra, LLC*, 269 F.3d 1321 (Fed. Cir. 2001) (the issue of what constitutes an offer for sale is governed by Federal common law for which the Uniform Commercial Code is a relevant source).

This instruction provides a discussion of the basic law, and leaves for oral argument the various factors tending to prove or disprove that an invention was on sale in any particular case.

AUTHORITIES

Pfaff v. *Wells Elecs., Inc.*, 525 U.S. 55 (1998); *Space Sys./Loral, Inc.* v. *Lockheed Martin Corp.*, 271 F.3d 1076, 1080 (Fed. Cir. 2001); *Scaltech, Inc.* v. *Retech/Tetra, LLC*, 269 F.3d 1321 (Fed. Cir. 2001); *Group One, Ltd.* v. *Hallmark Cards, Inc.*, 254 F.3d 1041, 1046–47 (Fed. Cir. 2001); *Robotic Vision Sys., Inc.* v. *View Eng'g, Inc.*, 249 F.3d 1307 (Fed. Cir. 2001); *Monon Corp.* v. *Stoughton Trailers, Inc.*, 239 F.3d 1253, 1257–61 (Fed. Cir. 2001); *Vanmoor* v. *Wal-Mart Stores, Inc.*, 201 F.3d 1363, 1366 (Fed. Cir. 2000); *STX, LLC* v. *Brine, Inc.*, 211 F.3d 588, 590 (Fed. Cir. 2000); *Zacharin* v. *United States*, 213 F.3d 1366, 1370 (Fed. Cir. 2000); *Brasseler, U.S.A.I, L.P.* v. *Stryker Sales Corp.*, 182 F.3d 888, 889 (Fed. Cir. 1999); *Cont'l Plastic Containers* v. *Owens Brockway Plastic Prods., Inc.*, 141 F.3d 1073, 1077 (Fed. Cir. 1998); *D.L. Auld Co.* v. *Chroma Graphics Corp.*, 714 F.2d 1144, 1147 (Fed. Cir. 1983); *W.L. Gore & Assocs., Inc.* v. *Garlock, Inc.*, 721 F.2d 1540, 1548–50 (Fed. Cir. 1983).

9.3.7   Experimental Use

Under certain circumstances, the public use, sale or offer for sale by the inventor or patent owner of the claimed invention is not prior art even if it was more than one year before the filing of the patent application. This occurs when the public use was for experimental rather than commercial purposes.

In order to qualify as experimentation, the public use, sale or offer for sale must be by, or for the benefit of, the patent owner or inventor, and must relate to the claimed features of the invention. It must also be for the purposes of technological development, not commercial gain. Any commercial gain that does occur must be merely incidental to the primary purpose of experimentation.

In this case, [plaintiff] asserts that its [use/sale/offer for sale] of _____ was an experimental use and, therefore, not prior art to the _____ patent claims.

NOTE

Experimental use of the claimed invention by the inventor or patent owner may provide an exception to the public use, sale or offer for sale prior art categories of 35 U.S.C. § 102(b). This exception "is based on the underlying policy of providing an inventor time to determine if the invention is suitable for its intended purpose, in effect, to reduce the invention to practice." *Lough* v. *Brunswick Corp.*, 86 F.3d 1113, 1120 (Fed. Cir. 1996). It has, therefore, been noted that an "experimental use can not occur after a reduction to practice." *Cont'l Plastic Containers* v. *Owens Brockway Plastic Prods., Inc.*, 141 F.3d 1073, 1079 (Fed. Cir. 1998). In addition, the experiments must test claimed features of the invention. Experiments performed on unclaimed features do not negate the on-sale bar. *EZ Dock, Inc.* v. *Schafer Sys., Inc.*, 276 F.3d 1347, 1353 (Fed. Cir. 2002).

In determining whether a use, offer to sell, or sale is "experimental," a fact-finder may consider such evidentiary factors as: (1) whether the inventor or patent owner received payment for the testing; (2) the length of the test period; (3) any agreement by the user to maintain the testing in confidence; (4) whether any record or progress report was made concerning the testing; (5) whether persons other than the inventor performed the testing; (6) the number of tests; (7) the length of the test period in relation to tests of similar devices; and (8) the extent of control the inventor maintained over the testing. *See Baxter Int'l, Inc.* v. *Cobe Labs., Inc.*, 88 F.3d 1054, 1060 (Fed. Cir. 1996); *Lough*, 86 F.3d at 1120.

The Court has noted that the last factor is "critically important, because, if the inventor has no control over the alleged experiments, he is not experimenting." *Lough*, 86 F.3d at 1120. The first factor, whether the inventor received payment, has also been found to be an important, but not dispositive, factual consideration. *Monon Corp.* v. *Stoughton Trailers, Inc.*, 239 F.3d 1253, 1260 (Fed. Cir. 2001); *Lough*, 86 F.3d at 1120.

The Federal Circuit has also held that the fact that a third party's public use may have been experimental in nature is irrelevant to determining the patent's validity. *Baxter Int'l, Inc.* v. *Cobe Labs., Inc.*, 88 F.3d 1054, 1060–61 (Fed. Cir. 1996) (holding that "public testing before the critical date by a third party for his own unique purposes of an invention previously reduced to practice and obtained from someone other than the patentee, when such testing is independent of and not controlled by the patentee, is an invalidating public use, not an experimental use"). The Court explained that the experimental nature of the third party's public use may benefit the third party if they were seeking a patent, but could not benefit the inventor. *Id.*

AUTHORITIES

Madey v. *Duke Univ.*, 307 F.3d 1351 (Fed. Cir. 2002); *New Railhead Mfg., L.L.C.* v. *Vermeer Mfg. Co.*, 298 F.3d 1290, 1297–99 (Fed. Cir. 2002); *Monon Corp.* v. *Stoughton Trailers, Inc.*, 239 F.3d 1253, 1257–61 (Fed. Cir. 2001); *Cont'l Plastic Containers* v. *Owens Brockway Plastic Prods., Inc.*, 141 F.3d 1073, 1079–80 (Fed. Cir. 1998); *Baxter Int'l Inc.* v. *Cobe Labs., Inc.*, 88 F.3d 1054,

1059–60 (Fed. Cir. 1996); *Lough v. Brunswick Corp.*, 86 F.3d 1113, 1119 (Fed. Cir. 1996), *reh'g en banc denied*, 103 F.3d 1517 (Fed. Cir. 1997); *W. Marine Elecs., Inc.* v. *Furuno Elec. Co.*, 764 F.2d 840, 846–47 (Fed. Cir. 1985).

9.3.8   Prior Art—Prior Printed Publication

Printed publications from anywhere in the world are prior art if the printed publications were published, either before the inventor made the claimed invention or more than one year before the application for the patent was filed.

A document is a printed publication if it was reasonably accessible to that portion of the public most likely to use it. It is not necessary that the publication be available to every member of the public. Thus, publications may include not only such things as books, periodicals or newspapers, but also publications that are not as widely available to the public, such as trade catalogues, journal articles or scholarly papers that are distributed or available to those skilled in the field of the invention.

The date that a printed publication becomes prior art is the date that it becomes available to the public. Published patent applications are printed publications as of their publication dates.

[If a printed publication was published more than one year before the application for the patent was filed, then that publication will be prior art, regardless of the date of invention for the patent claims. The date of invention is irrelevant to this category of prior art.]

In this case, [defendant] relies on _____ as a prior art printed publication to the _____ patent claims.

NOTE

The availability to the public of a document determines whether or not that document is a "printed publication" within the meaning of § 102. The Federal Circuit has defined "printed publication" as follows:

> The statutory phrase 'printed publication' has been interpreted to mean that before the critical date the reference must have been sufficiently accessible to the public interested in the art; dissemination and public accessibility are the keys to the legal determination whether a prior art reference was 'published.'"

In re Cronyn, 890 F.2d 1158, 1160 (Fed. Cir. 1989) (citation omitted).

The status of academic papers as prior art has been the subject of several Federal Circuit decisions. *See id.; In re Hall,* 781 F.2d 897 (Fed. Cir. 1986). In *Cronyn,* the applicant argued that a single cataloged thesis in one university library does not constitute sufficient accessibility to those skilled in the art. 890 F.2d at 1160. The Court disagreed, holding that the claims were unpatentable under 35 U.S.C. § 102(b) in light of the prior art thesis. The Court's decisions make clear that the focus of the inquiry is not on the number of copies available, but rather on whether the paper has been cataloged, by title or subject matter, so that one of skill in the art could gain access to it.

The Court has also made clear that "[e]vidence of routine business practice can be sufficient to prove that a reference was made accessible before a critical date." *Constant* v. *Advanced Micro-Devices Inc.,* 848 F.2d 1560, 1568 (Fed. Cir. 1988); *In re Hall,* 781 F.2d 897 (Fed. Cir. 1986).

AUTHORITIES

Mahurkar v. *C.R. Bard, Inc.,* 79 F.3d 1572, 1576 (Fed. Cir. 1996); *N. Telecom, Inc.* v. *Datapoint Corp.,* 908 F.2d 931, 936–37 (Fed. Cir. 1990); *In re Cronyn,* 890 F.2d 1158, 1159–61 (Fed. Cir. 1989); *Constant* v. *Advanced Micro-Devices, Inc.,* 848 F.2d 1560, 1568–69 (Fed. Cir. 1988); *In re Hall,* 781 F.2d 897, 899 (Fed. Cir. 1986); *Mass. Inst. of Tech.* v. *AB Fortia,* 774 F.2d 1104, 1108–09 (Fed. Cir. 1985); *In re Wyer,* 655 F.2d 221, 225 (C.C.P.A. 1981).

9.3.9   Prior Art—Prior Invention

An invention made by another person before the inventor on the patent made the invention is prior art to the patent claim, unless that other person abandoned, suppressed or concealed his or her invention.

As a general rule, the first person to reduce an invention to practice is said to be the first inventor. An invention is reduced to practice either when a patent application is filed or when the invention is made and shown to work for its intended purpose. Thus, if another person reduces an invention to practice before the inventor on the patent, then the reduction to practice by the other person will be prior art to the patent claims.

Let's consider an example. Mr. Smith has a patent on a table. He reduced his table to practice on April 1. Ms. Jones invents the same table. She built her table on March 1, one month before Mr. Smith reduced his table to practice. Ms. Jones' invention of the table is prior art to Mr. Smith's patent claims because Ms. Jones reduced her table to practice one month before Mr. Smith's reduction to practice.

[Include the following only if it is an issue in the case]:

There is, however, an important exception to this general rule. Someone who was first to conceive of an invention but reduced it to practice after someone else will be the first inventor if he or she was the first to conceive of the invention and he or she exercised "reasonable diligence" in reducing the invention to practice from a time beginning just before the other person's conception. Conception of an invention occurs when the inventor has formed the idea of how to make and use every aspect of the patented invention, and all that is required is that it be made without the need for any further inventive effort. Reasonable diligence means that the inventor worked continuously on reducing the invention to practice. Interruptions necessitated by the everyday problems and obligations of the inventor or those working with him or her do not prevent a finding of diligence.

Let's change our example slightly. Mr. Smith conceived of his table on February 1 and reduced it to practice on April 1. Ms. Jones conceived of the table on January 1, one month before Mr. Smith's conception, and built it on May 1, one month after Mr. Smith's reduction to practice. If Ms. Jones was reasonably diligent in building the table from the time just before Mr. Smith's February 1 conception up to the time that she built the table on May 1, she is the first inventor of the table and her invention is prior art to Mr. Smith's patent claims.

The final requirement for a prior invention to be prior art is that the prior inventor did not abandon, suppress or conceal his or her invention. Generally, an invention was not abandoned, suppressed or concealed if the invention was made public, sold or offered for sale, or otherwise used for a commercial purpose. The filing of a patent application that discloses the invention is evidence that the invention was not abandoned, suppressed or concealed.

In this case, [defendant] contends that _____ was a prior invention to the _____ patent claims.

NOTE

In general, an inventor is not entitled to a patent if a third party invented the claimed subject matter first. 35 U.S.C. § 102(g) (Supp. 2001). The test for determining when a prior art invention was made (i.e., conceived and reduced to practice) is the same as that used for determining the date of the invention claimed in the patent-in-suit. *See* Section 9.3.1, above.

An invention by a third party will be prior art to a claimed invention if the third party reduced the invention to practice before the patented invention was either actually or constructively reduced to practice. *Mycogen Plant Science, Inc.* v. *Monsanto Co.*, 243 F.3d 1316, 1332 (Fed. Cir. 2001). If, however, the third party reduced his or her invention after the patent's inventor, the third party's invention may nevertheless be prior art if he or she was the first to conceive of the invention, and exercised reasonable diligence in reducing the invention to practice from just before the patent inventor's conception until the third party's reduction to practice. *Mahurkar* v. *C.R. Bard, Inc.*, 79 F.3d 1572, 1578 (Fed. Cir. 1996); *Griffith* v. *Kanamaru*, 816 F.2d 624, 626 (Fed. Cir. 1987).

Reasonable diligence requires that an inventor continuously work on reducing the claimed invention to practice, without any extended periods of unexplainable delay. An inventor is, therefore, not required to devote his or her entire time to reducing the invention to practice. Moreover, a court may consider everyday problems and limitations encountered by the inventor as explanations for any delay. *Griffith* v. *Kanamaru*, 816 F.2d 624 (Fed. Cir. 1987); *Bey* v. *Kollonitsch*, 806 F.2d 1024 (Fed. Cir. 1986); *Gould* v. *Schawlow*, 53 C.C.P.A. 1403 (CCPA 1966). The particular factors relied on to support or dispute a claim of diligence are left for counsel's argument, and are not included in this instruction.

A third party's invention, even if prior to the claimed invention will not, however, be prior art if the third party "abandoned, suppressed or concealed" his or her invention. In *Apotex USA, Inc.* v. *Merck & Co.*, 254 F.3d 1031 (Fed. Cir. 2001), the Court discussed the burdens of proof governing a determination of whether or not a prior invention was abandoned, suppressed, or concealed under § 102(g). The Court stated that:

> [O]nce a challenger of a patent has proven by clear and convincing evidence that "the invention was made in this country by another inventor," 35 U.S.C. § 102(g), the burden of production shifts to the patentee to produce evidence sufficient to create a genuine issue of material fact as to whether the prior inventor has suppressed or concealed the invention. . . . Once the patentee has satisfied its burden of production, the party alleging invalidity under § 102(g) must rebut any alleged suppression or concealment with clear and convincing evidence to the contrary.

Id. at 1037. The burden of persuasion, however, remains with the party challenging the patent's validity. *Id.* at 1038.

Factors discussed in the case law in determining whether or not a prior invention has been abandoned, suppressed, or concealed, include whether or not (1) a patent application directed to the invention was filed, (2) the invention was described in a published document, or (3) the invention has been used publicly. *See Dow Chem. Co.* v. *Astro-Valcour, Inc.,* 267 F.3d 1334, 1341–43, (Fed. Cir. 2001); *Dunlop Holdings Ltd.* v. *Ram Golf Corp.,* 524 F.2d 33, 34 (7th Cir. 1975) (Justice Stevens, sitting by designation) (holding that the prior inventor's sale of golf balls with a patented cover made the benefits of the invention available to the public). The instruction refers to one of these factors—the presence of a patent application directed to the prior invention—but leaves the others to argument of counsel, as applicable.

AUTHORITIES

Dow Chem. Co. v. *Astro-Valcour, Inc.,* 267 F.3d 1334, 1341–43 (Fed. Cir. 2001); *Apotex USA, Inc.* v. *Merck & Co.,* 254 F.3d 1031 (Fed. Cir. 2001); *Mycogen Plant Sci., Inc.* v. *Monsanto Co.,* 243 F.3d 1316, 1330 (Fed. Cir. 2001); *Singh* v. *Brake,* 222 F.3d 1362, 1366–70 (Fed. Cir. 2000); *Genentech Inc.* v. *Chiron Corp.,* 220 F.3d 1345, 1351 (Fed. Cir. 2000); *Bruning* v. *Hirose,* 161 F.3d 681, 684–85 (Fed. Cir. 1998); *Cooper* v. *Goldfarb,* 154 F.3d 1321, 1326–31 (Fed. Cir. 1998); *Hyatt* v. *Boone,* 146 F.3d 1348, 1352–55 (Fed. Cir. 1998); *Estee Lauder Inc.* v. *L'Oreal, S.A.,* 129 F.3d 588, 593 (Fed. Cir. 1997); *Mahurkar* v. *C.R. Bard, Inc.,* 79 F.3d 1572, 1577–79 (Fed. Cir. 1996); *Checkpoint Sys.* v. *United States Int'l Trade Comm'n,* 54 F.3d 756, 761–63 (Fed. Cir. 1995); *Innovative Scuba Concepts, Inc.* v. *Feder Indus., Inc.,* 26 F.3d 1112, 1115–16 (Fed. Cir. 1994); *Griffith* v. *Kanamaru,* 816 F.2d 624, 626 (Fed. Cir. 1987); *Bey* v. *Kollonitsch,* 806 F.2d 1024, 1026 (Fed. Cir. 1986); *Dunlop Holdings Ltd.* v. *Ram Golf Corp.,* 524 F.2d 33, 34 (7th Cir. 1975); *Palmer* v. *Dudzik,* 481 F.2d 1377, 1385–87 (C.C.P.A. 1973); *Gould* v. *Schawlow,* 363 F.2d 908 (C.C.P.A. 1966).

9.3.10   Prior Art—Prior Patents and Patent Applications

An issued patent may be prior art to a patent claim under a number of different circumstances. First, a patent issued anywhere in the world, like a printed publication, may be prior art to a patent claim if the patent issued either before the inventor made the claimed invention, or more than one year before the application for the patent was filed.

[If a patent issued anywhere in the world more than one year before the application for the patent was filed, then that publication may be prior art, regardless of the date of invention of the claimed invention. The date of invention is irrelevant to this category of prior art.]

[A U.S. patent or published U.S. patent application may be prior art to a patent claim, even if the patent issued or the patent application was published after the date of invention of a claimed invention. This occurs when another person filed the patent application for the U.S. patent before the inventor made the claimed invention.]

In this case, [defendant] relies on _____ as a prior art [patent/patent application] to the _____ patent claims.

NOTE

In many countries, patent applications are published prior to the issuance of the patent. These published applications are considered "printed publications" under §§ 102(a) and (b). Prior to the recent patent law changes, a U.S. patent application was not published and, therefore, could not be prior art until it issued as a patent. Recent changes, however, bring the U.S. patent system in line with those of other countries. U.S. patent applications are now published eighteen months after filing. 35 U.S.C. § 122. These published applications may, therefore, be prior art under §§ 102(a) and (b) as of their publication date. These published applications may also be considered prior art under § 102(e)(1) (Supp. 2001), which was recently amended to state that "[a] person shall be entitled to a patent unless . . . [t]he invention was described in an *application* for patent, published under section 122(b), by another filed in the United States before the invention by the applicant for patent."

Patents may be prior art under §§ 102(a) and 102(b) as either being "patented" or "a printed publication." In the U.S., this distinction is meaningless because patents are published on the day that they issue. In certain foreign countries, however, a patent may issue prior to the patent being published. *See* 1 Irving Kayton, *Patent Practice* 4.7 (6th ed. 1995) (noting that France issues patents prior to publishing them). In these circumstances, patents may be prior art as of the day they issue.

AUTHORITIES

35 U.S.C. § 102(a), (b), and (e) (1984 & Supp. 2001); *Lamb-Weston, Inc.* v. *McCain Foods, Ltd.*, 78 F.3d 540, 545 (Fed. Cir. 1996); *In re Chu*, 66 F.3d 292, 296–97 (Fed. Cir. 1995); *In re Robertson*, 169 F.3d 743, 745 (Fed. Cir. 1999); *Baxter Int'l, Inc.* v. *Cobe Labs., Inc.*, 88 F.3d 1054, 1062 (Fed. Cir. 1996); *In re Bartfeld*, 925 F.2d 1450, 1452 (Fed. Cir. 1991).

9.4   Derivation

The patent laws require that the inventor on a patent be the true inventor of the invention covered by the patent claims. An inventor on a patent is not the true inventor if he "derived" the invention from someone else. An invention is said to be "derived" from another person if that other person conceived of the patented invention and communicated that conception to the inventor named on the patent. Conception of an invention occurs when the inventor has formed the idea of how to make and use every aspect of the patented invention, and all that is required is that it be made, without the need for further inventive effort. Derivation may be of the invention itself or of an obvious variation of the invention.

If an inventor derived the patented invention from someone else, then the patent claims covering the invention are invalid.

In this case, [defendant] contends that claims _____ of the _____ patent are invalid because the inventor on the _____ patent derived the invention of those claims from _____. If you find that [defendant] has proved that it is highly probable that the inventor on the _____ patent derived the invention covered by claims _____, then you must find that the claims are invalid.

NOTE

Under 35 U.S.C. § 102(f) (1984), an inventor is not entitled to a patent if he or she did not invent the subject matter of the claimed invention. In *OddzOn Prods., Inc.* v. *Just Toys, Inc.*, 122 F.3d 1396 (Fed. Cir. 1997), the Federal Circuit clarified that information derived by an inventor from another is prior art to claims encompassing that information, even though, unlike most other § 102 prior art categories, the derived information may never have been publicly available. *Id.* at 1401–02. The Court held that "subject matter derived from another not only is itself unpatentable to the party who derived it under section 102(f), but, when combined with other prior art, may make a resulting obvious invention unpatentable to

that party under a combination of sections 102(f) and 103."
Id. at 1403–04.

AUTHORITIES

Pannu v. *Iolab Corp.*, 155 F.3d 1344, 1349 (Fed. Cir. 1998); *Gambro Lundia AB* v. *Baxter Healthcare Corp.*, 110 F.3d 1573, 1576–78 (Fed. Cir. 1997); *Oddzon Prods., Inc.* v. *Just Toys, Inc.*, 122 F.3d 1396, 1401 (Fed. Cir. 1997); *Lamb-Weston, Inc.* v. *McCain Foods, Ltd.*, 78 F.3d 540, 544 (Fed. Cir. 1996); *Price* v. *Symsek*, 988 F.2d 1187, 1190 (Fed. Cir. 1993).

9.5   Anticipation—Introduction

A single item of prior art is said to "anticipate" a patent claim if the prior art item discloses, either expressly or inherently, all of the limitations of the claim. A prior art reference is deemed to disclose the subject matter set forth in the reference, as well as any subject matter that has been incorporated by reference. *See Ultradent Prods., Inc.* v. *Life-Like Cosmetics, Inc.,* 127 F.3d 1065, 1069 (Fed. Cir. 1997). Subject matter is inherently present in an item of prior art if "the disclosure is sufficient to show that the natural result flowing from the operation as taught would result in the performance of the questioned function." *Mehl/Biophile Int'l Corp.* v. *Milgraum,* 192 F.3d 1362, 1365 (Fed. Cir. 1999) (quoting *In re Oelrich,* 666 F.2d 578, 581 (CCPA 1981)).

In proving that any item of prior art inherently discloses a claim limitation, recourse to extrinsic evidence is appropriate. "Such evidence must make clear that the missing descriptive matter is necessarily present in the thing described in the reference, and that it would be so recognized by persons of ordinary skill." *Finnigan Corp.* v. *United States Int'l Trade Comm'n,* 180 F.3d 1354, 1365 (Fed. Cir. 1999); *Mehl/Biophile,* 192 F.3d at 1365 ("Inherency, however, may not be established by probabilities or possibilities. The mere fact that a certain thing may result from a given set of circumstances is not sufficient.").

For certain types of prior art (*e.g.,* patents and printed publications) to be anticipatory, the item of prior art must also be "enabling and describe the applicant's claimed invention sufficiently to have placed it in possession of a person of ordinary skill in the field of the invention." *In re Paulsen,* 30 F.3d 1475, 1479 (Fed. Cir. 1994). Non-enabling prior art cannot be anticipatory.

One way in which anticipation may be proved is by showing that the item of prior art infringes the patent claims. The oft-cited test states: "[t]hat which infringes if later in time anticipates if earlier." *Lewmar Marine, Inc.* v. *Barient, Inc.,* 827 F.2d 744, 747–48 (Fed. Cir. 1987). The Federal Circuit has clarified this test, however, by stating that "[a]ll infringements of a device do not 'anticipate.'" Rather, only literal infringements may be anticipations. The Court suggested that "the classic test must be modified to that which would literally infringe if later in time anticipates if earlier than the date of invention." *Id*.

9.6   Anticipation/Lack of Novelty

A person cannot obtain a patent on an invention if someone else has already made the same invention. In other words, the invention must be new. If an invention is not new, we say that it was "anticipated" by the prior art. An invention that is "anticipated" by the prior art is not entitled to patent protection. A party challenging the validity of a patent must prove anticipation by the highly probable standard.

In order for a patent claim to be anticipated by the prior art, each and every limitation of the claim must be present within a single item of prior art, whether that prior art is a publication, a prior patent, a prior invention, a prior public use or sale, or some other item of prior art. You may not find that the prior art anticipates a patent claim by combining two or more items of prior art.

[A printed publication or patent will not be an anticipation unless it contains a description of the invention covered by the patent claims that is sufficiently detailed to teach a skilled person how to make and use the invention without undue experimentation. That means that a person skilled in the field of the invention reading the printed publication or patent would be able to make and use the invention using only an amount of experimentation that is appropriate for the complexity of the field of the invention and for the level of expertise and knowledge of persons skilled in that field.]

In deciding whether or not a single item of prior art anticipates a patent claim, you should consider that which is expressly stated or present in the item of prior art, and also that which is inherently present. Something is inherent in an item of prior art if it is always present in the prior art or always results from the practice of the prior art, and if a person skilled in the field of the invention would understand that to be the case.

A prior public use by another may anticipate a patent claim, even if the use was accidental or was not appreciated by the other person. Thus, a prior public use may anticipate an invention even if the user did not intend to use the invention, or even realize he or she had done so.

In this case, defendant contends that claims _____ of the _____ patent are invalid because they are anticipated by _____. If you find that [defendant] has proved that it is highly probable that claims _____ are anticipated, then you must find that the claims are invalid.

AUTHORITIES

In re Cruciferous Sprout Litigation, 301 F.3d 1343, 1349–50 (Fed. Cir. 2002); *Ecolochem, Inc. v. S. Cal. Edison Co.*, 227 F.3d 1361, 1367–70 (Fed. Cir. 2000); *Atlas Powder Co. v. IRECO Inc.*, 190 F.3d 1342, 1346 (Fed. Cir. 1999); *Abbot Labs. v. Geneva Pharms., Inc.*, 182 F.3d 1315, 1318 (Fed. Cir. 1999); *Finnegan Corp. v. Int'l Trade Comm'n*, 180 F.3d 1354, 1364 (Fed. Cir. 1999); *C.R. Bard, Inc. v. M3 Sys., Inc.*, 157 F.3d 1340, 1349 (Fed. Cir. 1998); *W.L. Gore & Assocs., Inc. v. Garlock, Inc.*, 721 F.2d 1540, 1548 (Fed. Cir. 1983).

9.7   Obviousness—Introduction

In *Graham* v. *John Deere Co.*, 383 U.S. 1, 17–18 (1966), the Supreme Court set out the test for obviousness under 35 U.S.C. § 103. Obviousness is a question of law based on a number of factual determinations:

(1) the scope and content of the prior art are to be determined;

(2) differences between the prior art and the claims at issue are to be ascertained;

(3) the level of ordinary skill in the pertinent art; and

(4) the presence of objective indicia of non-obviousness ("secondary considerations"), such as commercial success, long-felt but unsolved needs, and failure of others to make the claimed invention.

Id. at 17–18. These *Graham* factors must always be considered when determining whether or not patent claims are invalid for obviousness. *See Ruiz* v. *Chance Co.*, 234 F.3d 654, 664 (Fed. Cir. 2000) (reversing the district court's holding of invalidity under 35 U.S.C. § 103 because the court failed to make explicit findings relating to the *Graham* factors).

The first factor requires the jury to identify the prior art that is relevant to the particular problem the claimed invention purports to solve. In considering the second factor, the jury must identify the limitations of the patent claims that are present in (and absent from) each of the items of prior art.

The third *Graham* factor, the level of ordinary skill in the art, requires that the jury determine the level of skill attributable to a hypothetical person of ordinary skill in the art. This hypothetical person is presumed to be aware of all of the prior art. In determining the level of skill in the art, the jury may consider:

(1) the types of problems encountered in the art;

(2) prior art solutions to those problems;

(3) the rapidity with which innovations are made in the art;

(4) the sophistication of the technology; and

(5) the educational level of workers in the field.

Ruiz, 234 F.3d at 666–67 (citations omitted).

The jury must determine whether or not it would have been obvious for this ordinary skilled worker to combine the prior art to come up with the invention claimed in the patent. Before it may find that the combination of prior art items would have been obvious, however, the jury must determine whether or not there was a suggestion or motivation in the prior art that would have led one of ordinary skill to make the combination. The jury may find the requisite suggestion or motivation to combine explicitly or implicitly:

(1) in the prior art references themselves;

(2) in the knowledge of those of ordinary skill in the art that certain references, or disclosures in those references, are of special interest or importance in the field; or

(3) from the nature of the problem to be solved, "leading inventors to look to references relating to possible solutions to that problem."

Ruiz, 234 F.3d at 665 (citations omitted).

The Federal Circuit has emphasized the importance of the motivation-to-combine requirement in obviousness. *See, e.g., Ecolochem, Inc. v. S. Cal. Edison Co.*, 227 F.3d 1361, 1371–72 (Fed. Cir. 2000), in which the Court reversed the district court's holding of obviousness because the court had failed to identify the motivation to combine the prior art references.

The last factor, collectively known as the objective indicia of non-obviousness, or secondary considerations, requires the jury to consider any evidence showing, for example, (1) that the claimed invention has achieved commercial success; (2) an unfilled, but long-felt need in the industry for the invention; (3) that others in the industry have copied the claimed invention; (4) that others in the industry have previously failed to solve the problem addressed by the claimed invention; and (5) that the claimed invention achieved unexpected results. The Federal Circuit has noted that this type of evidence "may often be the most probative and cogent evidence in the record." *Ruiz*, 234 F.3d at 667–68.

Although the question of obviousness or nonobviousness is ultimately a question of law, it has been a matter of routine for trial courts to permit the jury to reach the final conclusion of obviousness or nonobviousness based on its factual determinations. It may be preferred for the jury verdict form to set forth the jury's conclusions as to each of the factual determinations so that the appellate court may assess whether the jury's conclusion was based on appropriate fact-findings. *See, e.g., McGinley* v. *Franklin Sports, Inc.*, 262 F.3d 1339, 1358 (Fed. Cir. 2001) ("The issue presented in this appeal derives from the common, if unfortunate, practice of allowing the jury to render a general verdict on the ultimate legal conclusion of obviousness without requiring express findings on the underlying factual issues through a special verdict or special interrogatories under Fed. R. Civ. P. 49.") (Michel, J., dissenting opinion).

9.8 Obviousness

As I mentioned earlier, an inventor is not entitled to a patent if his or her invention would have been obvious to a person of ordinary skill in the field of the invention at the time the invention was made.

Unlike anticipation, obviousness may be shown by considering more than one item of prior art. The question is, would it have been obvious for a skilled person who knew of the prior art to make the claimed invention? If the answer to that question is yes, then the patent claims are invalid. [Defendant] has the burden of proving by the highly probable standard that claims _____ of the _____ patent are invalid for obviousness.

Obviousness is determined from the perspective of a person of ordinary skill in the field of the invention. The issue is not whether the claimed invention would have been obvious to you, to me as a judge, or to a genius in the field of the invention. Rather, the question is whether or not the invention would have been obvious to a person of ordinary skill in the field of the invention.

In deciding obviousness, you must avoid using hindsight; that is, you should not consider what is known today or what was learned from the teachings of the patent. You should not use the patent as a road map for selecting and combining items of prior art. You must put yourself in the place of a person of ordinary skill at the time the invention was made.

In determining whether or not these claims would have been obvious, you should make the following determinations:

First, what is the scope and content of the prior art?

Second, what differences, if any, are there between the invention of the claims of the patent and the prior art?

Third, what was the level of ordinary skill in the art at the time the invention was made?

Fourth, are there any objective indications of nonobviousness?

Against this background, you must decide whether or not the invention covered by the _____ patent claims would have been obvious.

I will now describe in more detail the specific determinations you must make in deciding whether or not the claimed invention would have been obvious.

AUTHORITIES

Graham v. *John Deere Co.*, 383 U.S. 1, 27–28 (1966); *LNP Eng'g Plastics, Inc.* v. *Miller Waste Mills, Inc.*, 275 F.3d 1347, 1359 (Fed. Cir. 2001); *Ruiz* v. *A.B. Chance Co.*, 234 F.3d 654, 662–68 (Fed. Cir. 2000); *Yamanouchi Pharm. Co.* v. *Danbury Pharmacal, Inc.*, 231 F.3d 1339, 1343–45 (Fed. Cir. 2000); *Brown & Williamson Tobacco Corp.* v. *Philip Morris Inc.*, 229 F.3d 1120, 1124–31 (Fed. Cir. 2000); *Ecolochem, Inc.* v. *S. Cal. Edison Co.*, 227 F.3d 1361, 1371–81 (Fed. Cir. 2000); *In re Kotzab*, 217 F.3d 1365, 1369 (Fed. Cir. 2000); *In re Dembiczak*, 175 F.3d 994, 998–1000 (Fed. Cir. 1999); *In re Rouffet*, 149 F.3d 1350, 1355–56 (Fed. Cir. 1998); *In re Deuel*, 51 F.3d 1552, 1557–60 (Fed. Cir. 1995); *Orthokinetics, Inc.* v. *Safety Travel Chairs, Inc.*, 806 F.2d 1565, 1574–75 (Fed. Cir. 1986).

9.8.1 The Scope and Content of the Prior Art

Determining the scope and content of the prior art means that you should determine what is disclosed in the prior art relied on by [defendant]. You must decide whether this prior art was reasonably relevant to the particular problem the inventor was attempting to solve in making the invention covered by the patent claims. Such relevant prior art includes prior art in the field of the invention, and also prior art from other fields that a person of ordinary skill would look to when attempting to solve the problem.

AUTHORITIES

Graham v. *John Deere Co.*, 383 U.S. 1, 27–28 (1966); *Ruiz* v. *A.B. Chance Co.*, 234 F.3d 654, 664–65 (Fed. Cir. 2000); *In re Kotzab*, 217 F.3d 1365, 1369 (Fed. Cir. 2000); *SIBIA Neurosciences, Inc.* v. *Cadus Pharm. Corp.*, 225 F.3d 1349, 1356–57 (Fed. Cir. 2000); *In re Dembiczak*, 175 F.3d 994, 999–1000 (Fed. Cir. 1999); *In re Rouffet*, 149 F.3d 1350, 1355–56 (Fed. Cir. 1998); *Monarch Knitting Mach. Corp.* v. *Sulzer Morat GmbH*, 139 F.3d 877, 881–83 (Fed. Cir. 1998); *Wang Lab.* v. *Toshiba Corp.*, 993 F.2d 858, 863 (Fed. Cir. 1993); *Ryko Mfg. Co.* v. *Nu-Star, Inc.*, 950 F.2d 714, 716–17 (Fed. Cir. 1991).

9.8.2 Differences between the Invention of the Claims and the Prior Art

In determining the differences between the invention covered by the patent claims and the prior art, you should not look at the individual differences in isolation. You must consider the claimed invention as a whole and determine whether or not it would have been obvious in light of all of the prior art.

In deciding whether to combine what is described in various items of prior art, you should keep in mind that there must be some motivation or suggestion for a skilled person to make the combination covered by the patent claims. You should also consider whether or not someone reading the prior art would be discouraged from following the path taken by the inventor.

AUTHORITIES

Graham v. *John Deere Co.*, 383 U.S. 1, 27–28 (1966); *Ruiz* v. *A.B. Chance Co.*, 234 F.3d 654, 664–65 (Fed. Cir. 2000); *Yamanouchi Pharm. Co.* v. *Danbury Pharmacal, Inc.*, 231 F.3d 1339, 1343–45 (Fed. Cir. 2000); *Ecolochem, Inc.* v. *S. Cal. Edison Co.*, 227 F.3d 1361, 1371–81 (Fed. Cir. 2000); *In re Kotzab*, 217 F.3d 1365, 1369 (Fed. Cir. 2000); *Winner Int'l Royalty Corp.* v. *Wang*, 202 F.3d 1340, 1349 (Fed. Cir. 2000); *In re Dembiczak*, 175 F.3d 994, 998–1000 (Fed. Cir. 1999); *Monarch Knitting Mach. Corp.* v. *Sulzer Morat GmbH*, 139 F.3d 877, 881–83 (Fed. Cir. 1998); *Nyko Mfg. Co.* v. *Nu-Star, Inc.*, 950 F.2d 714, 717 (Fed. Cir. 1991).

9.8.3 Level of Ordinary Skill

Obviousness is determined from the perspective of a person of ordinary skill in the art. This person is presumed to know all of the prior art, not just what the inventor may have known. When faced with a problem, this ordinary skilled person is able to apply his or her experience and ability to the problem and also to look to any available prior art to help solve the problem.

Factors to consider in determining the level of ordinary skill in the art include the educational level and experience of people working in the field, the types of problems faced by workers in the art and the solutions found to those problems, and the sophistication of the technology in the field.

AUTHORITIES

Graham v. *John Deere Co.*, 383 U.S. 1, 27–28 (1966); *Ruiz* v. *A.B. Chance Co.*, 234 F.3d 654, 666–67 (Fed. Cir. 2000); *Brown & Williamson Tobacco Corp.* v. *Philip Morris Inc.*, 229 F.3d 1120, 1125 (Fed. Cir. 2000); *SIBIA Neurosciences, Inc.* v. *Cadus Pharm. Corp.*, 225 F.3d 1349, 1356–57 (Fed. Cir. 2000); *In re Dembiczak*, 175 F.3d 994, 998–99 (Fed. Cir. 1999); *Al-Site Corp.* v. *VSI Int'l, Inc.*, 174 F.3d 1308, 1323–25 (Fed. Cir. 1999); *In re Dance*, 160 F.3d 1339, 1343 (Fed. Cir. 1998); *Ryko Mfg. Co.* v. *Nu-Star, Inc.*, 950 F.2d 714, 718–19 (Fed. Cir. 1991).

9.8.4   Objective Indications Concerning Obviousness

You also must consider what are referred to as objective indications of nonobviousness. Some of these indications of nonobviousness are:

1. Commercial success of products covered by the patent claims or made by a process covered by the patent claims.

2. A long-felt need for the invention.

3. Failed attempts by others to make the invention.

4. Copying of the invention by others in the field.

5. Unexpected results achieved by the invention.

6. Praise of the invention by the infringer or others in the field.

7. The taking of licenses under the patent by others.

8. Expressions of surprise by experts and those skilled in the art at the making of the invention.

9. The patentee proceeded contrary to the accepted wisdom of the prior art.

The presence of any of these objective indications may suggest that the invention was not obvious. These objective indications are only relevant to obviousness if there is a connection, or nexus, between them and the invention covered by the patent claims. For example, commercial success is relevant to obviousness only if the success of the product is related to a feature of the patent claims. If the commercial success is the result of something else, such as innovative marketing, and not to a patented feature, then you should not consider it to be an indication of nonobviousness.

AUTHORITIES

Graham v. *John Deere Co.*, 383 U.S. 1, 27–28 (1966); *Ruiz* v. *A.B. Chance Co.*, 234 F.3d 654, 667–68 (Fed. Cir. 2000); *Brown & Williamson Tobacco Corp.* v. *Philip Morris Inc.*, 229 F.3d 1120, 1129–31 (Fed. Cir. 2000); *SIBIA Neurosciences, Inc.* v. *Cadus*

Pharm. Corp., 225 F.3d 1349, 1356–57 (Fed. Cir. 2000); *In re Dance*, 160 F.3d 1339, 1343 (Fed. Cir. 1998); *Ryko Mfg. Co.* v. *Nu-Star, Inc.*, 950 F.2d 714, 718–19 (Fed. Cir. 1991).

9.8.5 Determination of Obviousness

[Defendant] contends that the invention claimed in claims
_____ of the _____ patent would have been obvious to a
person of ordinary skill in the field of the invention at the
time the invention was made in light of the _____ item
of prior art combined with _____. If you find that [defendant] has proved obviousness by the highly probable standard, then you must find that the claims are invalid for
obviousness.

Chapter Ten
Inequitable Conduct—Introduction

10.   Inequitable Conduct—Introduction

Inequitable conduct is a judicially created defense, based on the principal that a patent obtained through misrepresentation or omission of material information should not be enforceable. Inequitable conduct has been defined in the case law as including "affirmative misrepresentations of a material fact, failure to disclose material information, or submission of false material information, coupled with an intent to deceive." *PerSeptive Biosystems, Inc.* v. *Pharmacia Biotech, Inc.*, 225 F.3d 1315, 1318 (Fed. Cir. 2000).

There is no set formula for determining the materiality of a misrepresentation or omission and the intent to deceive. Materiality and intent must be balanced to determine whether, in light of all of the circumstances, the patent owner's conduct was sufficient to render the patent unenforceable. *Li Second Family Ltd. P'ship* v. *Toshiba Corp.*, 231 F.3d 1373, 1378 (Fed. Cir. 2000). Thus, for example, if misrepresented or withheld information is highly material to patentability, a lower threshold of intent will be required to support a conclusion of inequitable conduct, and vice versa. *Id.*

The Federal Circuit has recognized that direct evidence of intent will rarely be available, and that an intent to deceive must be inferred from the circumstances:

> Intent need not be proven by direct evidence; it is most often proven by a showing of acts, the natural consequences of which are presumably intended by the actor. Generally, intent must be inferred from the facts and circumstances surrounding the applicant's conduct.

Molins PLC v. *Textron, Inc.*, 48 F.3d 1172, 1180–81 (Fed. Cir. 1995) (citations omitted).

For example, the high materiality of the withheld information and the absence of a credible explanation of why it was not disclosed leads to an inference of an intent to deceive. *Critikon, Inc.* v. *Becton Dickinson Vascular Access, Inc.*, 120 F.3d 1253, 1259 (Fed. Cir. 1997) ("Given the materiality and the failure at any point to offer a good faith explanation of the pattern of nondisclosure, an intent to mislead may be inferred."); *see also Baxter Int'l, Inc.* v. *McGaw, Inc.*, 149 F.3d 1321 (Fed. Cir. 1998) (high materiality of withheld prior art coupled with absence of evidence of mitigating good faith led to inference of intent to deceive). Similarly, an intent to deceive may be inferred from the submission of false or incomplete declarations to the Patent Office. *Refac Int'l, Ltd.* v. *Lotus Dev. Corp.*, 81 F.3d 1576 (Fed. Cir. 1996) (submission of declarations that omitted information about the relationship between the declarant and patentee evinced an intent to deceive).

Because inequitable conduct is an equitable doctrine, it may be reserved for the Court. The Federal Circuit has made plain, however, that it is not an abuse of discretion for the district court to permit the jury to decide inequitable conduct. *Hebert* v. *Lisle Corp.*, 99 F.3d 1109 (Fed. Cir. 1996).

> There are a variety of ways in which the district court may choose to handle the issue of inequitable conduct during a jury trial, as the Federal Circuit has recognized. Some courts have reserved the entire issue of inequitable conduct unto themselves; some have submitted special interrogatories to the jury on the facts of materiality and intent; and some have instructed the jury to find and weigh the facts of materiality and intent and decide the ultimate question of inequitable conduct, as in the case at bar.

Id. at 1114; *see also Juicy Whip, Inc.* v. *Orange Bang, Inc.*, 292 F.3d 728, 737 (Fed. Cir. 2002).

10.1   Inequitable Conduct—in General

After a patent application is filed, it is assigned to an Examiner, who examines the application and attempts to determine whether or not the application and the claims meet all of the requirements of the patent laws.

In conducting this examination, the Examiner must consider the description of the invention in the application, which may involve a highly technical subject matter, and search for and consider the prior art. The Examiner has only a limited amount of time and resources available and, therefore, must rely on information provided by the applicant with respect to the technical field of the invention and the prior art.

Because the Patent and Trademark Office must rely on the patent applicant for information, applicants for patents have a duty of honesty and good faith in their dealings with the Patent and Trademark Office. Persons who have this duty include the inventor named on the patent application, persons who represent the inventor before the Patent and Trademark Office, and other persons involved in a substantial way with the application.

This duty of honesty and good faith exists from the time the application is filed and continues for the entire time that an application is pending before the Patent and Trademark Office. It requires that the applicant, the applicant's representatives, and others involved in a substantial way with the application fully disclose to the Patent and Trademark Office all information of which they are aware that is material to examination of the application, including all material prior art. I will explain to you in a moment how you may determine whether or not information is material.

Intentional failure to fulfill this duty of honesty and good faith is called inequitable conduct. When inequitable conduct occurs during the course of obtaining a patent, the patent is unenforceable. This means that the patent owner may not prevent others from using the invention covered by the claims of the patent and may not collect damages for patent infringement.

[Defendant] has the burden of proving inequitable conduct by the highly probable standard. [Defendant] must prove that the inventor, the inventor's representative, or someone involved in a substantial way with the application withheld or misrepresented information that was material to the examination of the _____ patent application, and that such person or persons acted with an intent to deceive or mislead the Patent Examiner.

I will now explain to you the requirements of materiality and intent. I will then explain how you should balance any materiality and intent that you find in order for you to determine whether or not there was inequitable conduct.

AUTHORITIES

37 C.F.R. § 1.56 (2001); *Juicy Whip, Inc. v. Orange Bang, Inc.*, 292 F.3d 728, 737 (Fed. Cir. 2002); *PerSeptive Biosystems, Inc. v. Pharmacia Biotech, Inc.*, 225 F.3d 1315, 1318 (Fed. Cir. 2000); *Critikon, Inc. v. Becton Dickinson Vascular Access, Inc.*, 120 F.3d 1253, 1256–57 (Fed. Cir. 1997); *N. Telecom, Inc. v. Datapoint Corp.*, 908 F.2d 931, 938–39 (Fed. Cir. 1990); *Kingsdown Med. Consultants, Ltd. v. Hollister, Inc.*, 863 F.2d 867, 876 (Fed. Cir. 1988) (*en banc*); *KangaROOS U.S.A., Inc. v. Caldor, Inc.*, 778 F.2d 1571, 1576–77 (Fed. Cir. 1985).

10.2   Materiality

In considering the issue of materiality, you must first determine whether or not information was withheld from or misrepresented to the Patent and Trademark Office. If you find that the inventor, the inventor's representative, or others involved in a substantial way with the application withheld or misrepresented information when applying for the _____ patent, you must then determine whether or not that information was material.

[Information is material if it establishes, either alone or in combination with other information, that a claim of the patent application more likely than not does not meet one of the requirements for a patent, such as the requirements that a patented invention be new, useful and nonobvious. Information is also material if it refutes or is inconsistent with information provided or arguments made to persuade the Examiner that the invention is entitled to patent protection. Information that is cumulative of, that is, that adds little to other information the Examiner already had, is not material.]

[Information is material if there is a substantial likelihood that a reasonable Patent Examiner would consider it important in deciding whether or not to allow the application to issue as a patent.]

You must next consider whether or not there was an intent to mislead or deceive the Patent and Trademark Office.

NOTE

The standard articulated in the Patent Office rules for determining materiality (37 C.F.R. § 1.56) changed in January 1992. The new standard is set forth in the second full paragraph above, and the pre-1992 standard is set forth in the third full paragraph.

The Federal Circuit has applied the pre-1992 standard to cases in which the application for the patent-in-suit was prosecuted before the rule change. *PerSeptive Biosystems, Inc.* v. *Pharmacia Biotech, Inc.*, 225 F.3d 1315 (Fed. Cir. 2000); *Baxter*

Int'l, Inc. v. *Baxter Healthcare Corp.*, 149 F.3d 1321 (Fed. Cir. 1998). The Court has yet to decide "whether it should adhere to the preexisting standard for inequitable conduct in prosecution occurring after the effective date of the new rule." *See Dayco Products, Inc.* v. *Total Containment, Inc.*, 329 F.3d 1358 (Fed. Cir. 2003) ("Because we conclude that the outcome of this appeal would be the same under either materiality standard, we leave for another day a final disposition of this issue.").

AUTHORITIES

37 C.F.R. § 1.56 (2000); *Dayco Products, Inc.* v. *Total Containment, Inc.*, 329 F.3d 1358 (Fed. Cir. 2003); *Li Second Family Ltd. P'ship* v. *Toshiba Corp.*, 231 F.3d 1373, 1379–80 (Fed. Cir. 2000); *PerSeptive Biosystems, Inc.* v. *Pharmacia Biotech, Inc.*, 225 F.3d 1315, 1321–22 (Fed. Cir. 2000); *Life Tech., Inc.* v. *Clontech Labs., Inc.*, 224 F.3d 1320, 1324–26 (Fed. Cir. 2000); *Union Oil Co. of Cal.* v. *Atl. Richfield Co.*, 208 F.3d 989 (Fed. Cir. 2000); *Semiconductor Energy Lab. Co.* v. *Samsung Elecs. Co.*, 204 F.3d 1368, 1374 (Fed. Cir. 2000); *Elk Corp. of Dallas* v. *GAF Bldg. Materials Corp.*, 168 F.3d 28, 31 (Fed. Cir. 1999); *Baxter Int'l, Inc.* v. *McGaw, Inc.*, 149 F.3d 1321 (Fed. Cir. 1998); *Critikon, Inc.* v. *Becton Dickinson Vascular Access, Inc.*, 120 F.3d 1253, 1257–59 (Fed. Cir. 1997); *Litton Sys., Inc.* v. *Honeywell, Inc.*, 87 F.3d 1559, 1570–71 (Fed. Cir. 1996); *Molins PLC* v. *Textron, Inc.*, 48 F.3d 1172, 1178–79 (Fed. Cir. 1995).

10.3   Intent

Evidence relevant to the question of intent to deceive or mislead the Patent and Trademark Office includes any direct evidence of intent, as well as evidence from which intent may be inferred. The patent law recognizes that direct evidence of an actual intent to deceive or mislead is rarely available. You may, however, infer intent from conduct. That means you may conclude that a person intended the foreseeable results of his or her actions. You should decide whether or not to infer an intent to deceive or mislead based on the totality of the circumstances, including the nature of the conduct and evidence of the absence or presence of good faith.

AUTHORITIES

Li Second Family Ltd. P'ship v. *Toshiba Corp.*, 231 F.3d 1373, 1379–80 (Fed. Cir. 2000); *PerSeptive Biosystems, Inc.* v. *Pharmacia Biotech, Inc.*, 225 F.3d 1315, 1321–22 (Fed. Cir. 2000); *Semiconductor Energy Lab. Co.* v. *Samsung Elecs. Co.*, 204 F.3d 1368, 1374 (Fed. Cir. 2000); *Critikon, Inc.* v. *Becton Dickinson Vascular Access, Inc.*, 120 F.3d 1253, 1257–59 (Fed. Cir. 1997); *Refac Int'l Ltd.* v. *Lotus Dev. Corp.*, 81 F.3d 1576 (Fed. Cir. 1996); *Molins PLC* v. *Textron, Inc.*, 48 F.3d 1172, 1180–81 (Fed. Cir. 1995); *Kingsdown Med. Consultants, Ltd.* v. *Hollister, Inc.*, 863 F.2d 867, 876 (Fed. Cir. 1988) (*en banc*).

10.4 Balancing of Materiality and Intent

If you find that [defendant] has proved that it is highly probable that material information was withheld or misrepresented and that there was an intent to deceive or mislead the Patent Examiner, you must then balance the degree of materiality and the degree of intent to determine whether or not the evidence is sufficient to establish that there was inequitable conduct.

The higher the materiality of the withheld or misrepresented information is, the lower the intent needed to establish inequitable conduct.

AUTHORITIES

Li Second Family Ltd. P'ship v. *Toshiba Corp.*, 231 F.3d 1373, 1378 (Fed. Cir. 2000); *Baxter Int'l, Inc.* v. *McGaw, Inc.*, 149 F.3d 1321, 1327 (Fed. Cir. 1998); *Critikon, Inc.* v. *Becton Dickinson Vascular Access, Inc.*, 120 F.3d 1253, 1256 (Fed. Cir. 1997); *Molins PLC* v. *Textron, Inc.*, 48 F.3d 1172, 1178 (Fed. Cir. 1995); *FMC Corp.* v. *Manitowoc Co.*, 835 F.2d 1411, 1416 (Fed. Cir. 1987); *Am. Hoist & Derrick Co* v. *Sowa & Sons, Inc.*, 725 F.2d 1350, 1363–64 (Fed. Cir. 1984).

Chapter Eleven
Damages—Introduction

11.   Damages—Introduction

35 U.S.C. § 284 states that:

> Upon finding for the claimant the court shall award the claimant damages adequate to compensate for the infringement but in no event less than a reasonable royalty for the use made of the invention by the infringer, together with interest and costs as fixed by the court.

This section sets forth the lower limit of damages for patent infringement, *i.e.*, a patent owner is entitled to at least a reasonable royalty. It does not, however, set forth an upper limit. Rather, the statute requires that the damages be "adequate" to compensate for the infringement. The goal is to put the patent owner in the position it would have been in "but for" the infringement. *Pall Corp.* v. *Micron Separations, Inc.*, 66 F.3d 1211 (Fed. Cir. 1995).

The case law further defines the types of damages that a patent owner may recover for infringement and the manner in which they are determined. For example, in *Rite-Hite Corp.* v. *Kelley Co.*, 56 F.3d 1538, 1546 (Fed. Cir. 1995) (*en banc*), the Federal Circuit held that the test for damages under § 284 "is not solely a 'but for' test in the sense that an infringer must compensate a patentee for any and all damages that proceed from the act of patent infringement." Rather, "the balance between full compensation . . . and the reasonable limits of liability encompassed by general principles of law can best be viewed in terms of reasonable, objective forseeability." *Id.* A patent owner must, therefore, demonstrate that "the asserted injury is of the type for which he may be compensated." *Id.*

In *Rite-Hite*, the Court explained that certain types of injuries, even if the direct result of the infringement, such as a patent owner suffering a heart attack or the value of a patent owner corporation's shares decreasing, are too remote to warrant compensation.

The parties may want to consider holding separate trials on the issues of liability and damages to simplify the issue for the jury and in the interests of judicial economy. Moreover, courts have recognized that there is a potential for prejudice to the defendant if a jury hears summations and instructions regarding damages before a determination of liability has been made. *E.g., Johns Hopkins Univ.* v. *Cellpro,* 34 USPQ2d 1276 (D. Del. 1995). By limiting party summations and jury instructions to the issue of liability only, the potential for jury prejudice against the defendant may be minimized, and only after a finding of liability will the issue of damages need to be decided. It is solely within the trial court's discretion to determine whether factors in the particular case, including convenience of the parties, avoidance of prejudice, and judicial economy, weigh in favor of separation of liability and damages issues for trial. Fed. R. Civ. P. 42(b).

11.1   Damages—in General

I have now instructed you as to the law governing [plaintiff's] claims of patent infringement and [defendant's] claims of invalidity [and unenforceability]. If you find that [defendant] has infringed a valid [and enforceable] claim of the _____ patent, then you must determine what damages [defendant] must pay to [plaintiff] for that infringement. If, on the other hand, you find that [defendant] has not infringed a valid [and enforceable] claim of the _____ patent, then [plaintiff] is not entitled to any damages, and you should not make any findings about damages.

The fact that I am instructing you about damages does not mean that [plaintiff] is or is not entitled to recover damages. I am expressing no opinion one way or the other. These instructions are only to guide you in case you find that [defendant] infringed a valid [and enforceable] claim of the patent.

11.2   Compensatory Patent Damages

If you find that any claim of the _____ patent is both valid and infringed, then the patent owner is entitled to damages adequate to compensate for the infringement. These damages may not be less than what a reasonable royalty would be for the use made of the invention by the infringer. In determining damages, you must decide how much financial harm the patent owner has suffered by reason of the infringement. You must decide the amount of money that the patent owner would have made had the infringer not infringed.

Damages are only to compensate [plaintiff], to put [plaintiff] into the position it would have been in if [defendant] had not infringed. You may not add anything to the amount of damages to punish [defendant], or to set an example.

AUTHORITIES

35 U.S.C. § 284 (2001); *Grain Processing Corp.* v. *Am. Maize-Prod. Co.*, 185 F.3d 1341, 1349 (Fed. Cir. 1999); *Maxwell* v. *J. Baker, Inc.*, 86 F.3d 1098, 1108–09 (Fed. Cir. 1996); *Pall Corp.* v. *Micron Separations, Inc.*, 66 F.3d 1211 (Fed. Cir. 1995); *Rite-Hite Corp.* v. *Kelley Co.*, 56 F.3d 1538, 1545 (Fed. Cir. 1995) (*en banc*).

11.3   Notice Requirement for Patents with Product Claims

[Plaintiff] can recover damages for infringement that occurred only after [plaintiff] gave notice of its patent rights. It is [plaintiff's] burden to prove by the more probable than not standard that it gave notice.

[Plaintiff] can give notice in two ways. The first way is to give notice to the public in general. [Plaintiff] can do this by placing the word "patent" or the abbreviation "PAT." with the number of the patent on substantially all the products it sold that included the patented invention. [The [plaintiff's] licensees who use the patented invention must also mark substantially all of their products that include the patented invention with the patent number.] This type of notice is effective from the date [plaintiff] [and its licensees] began to mark substantially all of [its/their] products that use the patented invention with the patent number. If [plaintiff] [and its licensees] did not mark substantially all of [its/their] products that use the patented invention with the patent number, then [plaintiff] did not provide notice in this way.]

A second way [plaintiff] can provide notice of its patent is to tell [defendant] that [defendant] is infringing the _____ patent and to identify [defendant's] product that was infringing. This type of notice is effective from the time it is given.

As I said, [plaintiff] may recover damages only from the time it gave notice of its patent, either by the marking of products or by telling [defendant] of its infringement. If you find that [plaintiff] did not do either of these before beginning this lawsuit, then [plaintiff] can only recover damages for infringement that occurred after it sued [defendant] on [date].

NOTE

Use this instruction when the patent owner or its licensee is asserting product claims and sells a product that is covered by the asserted product claims.

35 U.S.C. § 287(a) states:

> Patentees, and persons making, offering for sale, or selling within the United States any patented article for or under them, or importing any patented article into the United States, may give notice to the public that the same is patented, either by fixing thereon the word "patent" or the abbreviation "pat.", together with the number of the patent, or when, from the character of the article, this can not be done, by fixing to it, or to the package wherein one or more of them is contained, a label containing a like notice. In the event of failure so to mark, no damages shall be recovered by the patentee in any action for infringement, except on proof that the infringer was notified of the infringement and continued to infringe thereafter, in which event damages may be recovered only for infringement occurring after such notice. Filing of an action for infringement shall constitute such notice.

The purpose of this section is to encourage the patent owner to provide notice to the public of the patent and to minimize the risk of unintentional infringement. Thus, under § 287(a), damages will begin to accrue only after a patent owner has provided an accused infringer with notice of the patent. Notice of the patent may be provided constructively, by marking the patented invention in accordance with § 287(a), or actually, by notifying the infringer of its infringement. A patent owner choosing to mark the patented invention must ensure that the patented invention is consistently and continuously marked, and that persons authorized to make or sell the patented invention, such as licensees, also comply with the requirements of § 287(a). *Maxwell* v. *J. Baker*, 86 F.3d 1098, 1111 (Fed.Cir. 1996).

The Federal Circuit has recognized that, in situations where third parties are making and selling the patented invention, "it is often more difficult for a patent [owner] to ensure compliance with the marking provisions." *Id*. To combat this problem, the Court has adopted a "rule of reason" approach; that is, whether "the patent [owner] made reasonable efforts to ensure compliance with the marking requirements." *Id*. at 1112.

In general, the marking requirement only applies when there is a tangible item that can be marked. *Am. Med. Systems Inc.* v. *Medical Eng'g Corp.*, 6 F.3d 1523, 1538–39 (Fed. Cir. 1993).

The marking requirement, therefore, does not apply when a patent owner does not make or sell the patented invention. Likewise, the marking requirement does not apply when a patent contains only process claims. *Id.*

When a patent contains both product and process claims, and there is a tangible item that can be marked, a patent owner must comply with § 287(a) if both the product and process claims are asserted. *Id.* at 1538; *see also Devices for Med. Inc.* v. *Boehl*, 822 F.2d 1062, 1066 (Fed. Cir. 1987). It is unclear, however, whether a patentee can avoid the requirements of § 287(a) by only asserting the process claims. *Compare Boehl*, 822 F.2d at 1066, with *Hanson* v. *Alpine Valley Ski Area, Inc.*, 718 F.2d 1075, 1083 (Fed. Cir. 1983) and *Loral Fairchild Corp.* v. *Victor Co. of Japan, Ltd.*, 906 F. Supp. 813, 817 (E.D.N.Y. 1995).

If a patent owner chooses not to mark the patented invention, the patent owner's damages will begin to accrue only after the patent owner provides the accused infringer with actual notice of the alleged infringement. The Federal Circuit has held that "[a]ctual notice requires the affirmative communication of a specific charge of infringement by a specific accused product or device." *Amsted Indus. Inc.* v. *Buckeye Steel Castings Co.*, 24 F.3d 178, 187 (Fed. Cir. 1994). However, "the requirement of a specific charge of infringement set forth in *Amsted* does not mean that the patent [owner] must make an unqualified charge of infringement." *Gart* v. *Logitech, Inc.*, 254 F.3d 1334, 1346 (Fed. Cir. 2001). In *Gart*, the Court reviewed the notification letter in its entirety to determine whether it objectively conveyed the patent owner's belief that the accused products infringed. In making this determination, "[t]he correct approach to determining notice under section 287 must focus on the action of the patent [owner], not the knowledge or understanding of the infringer." *Amsted*, 24 F.3d at 188.

Moreover, in order for a notification letter to be sufficient for the purposes of § 287(a), the patent owner must send it as a result of an affirmative act. *See Lans* v. *Digital Equipment Corp.*,

252 F.3d 1320, 1327–28 (Fed. Cir. 2001) (holding that the notification letters sent to the accused infringer were insufficient because the letters were not sent by the patent owner and did not accurately identify the patent owner).

AUTHORITIES

35 U.S.C. § 287 (2001); *Gart v. Logitech, Inc.*, 254 F.3d 1334, 1346 (Fed. Cir. 2001); *Lans v. Digital Equipment Corp.*, 252 F.3d 1320, 1327–28 (Fed. Cir. 2001); *Crystal Semiconductor Corp. v. Tritech Microelecs. Int'l, Inc.*, 246 F.3d 1336, 1353 (Fed. Cir. 2001); *Nike Inc. v. Wal-Mart Stores*, 138 F.3d 1437, 1443–44 (Fed. Cir. 1998); *Maxwell v. J. Baker, Inc.*, 86 F.3d 1098, 1108–09 (Fed. Cir. 1996); *Amsted Indus. Inc. v. Buckeye Steel Castings Co.*, 24 F.3d 178, 187 (Fed. Cir. 2001); *Am. Med. Sys. v. Medical Eng'g Corp.*, 6 F.3d 1523, 1534 (Fed. Cir. 1993); *Devices for Med., Inc. v. Boehl*, 822 F.2d 1062, 1066 (Fed. Cir. 1987); *Hanson v. Alpine Valley Ski Area, Inc.*, 718 F.2d 1075, 1083 (Fed. Cir. 1983); *Loral Fairchild, Corp. v. Victor Co. of Japan, Ltd.*, 906 F.Supp. 813, 817 (E.D.N.Y. 1995).

11.4　Two Types of Damages—Lost Profits and Reasonable Royalty

There are two types of damages for patent infringement.

The first type of patent damages is lost profits. Briefly, lost profits damages compensate the patent owner for the additional profits that it would have made if the accused infringer had not infringed. You may hear this referred to as the "but for" test. I will discuss lost profits in more detail shortly.

The second type of patent damages is called reasonable royalty. I will also discuss reasonable royalty later in more detail. Generally, a reasonable royalty is defined by the patent laws as the reasonable amount that someone wanting to use the patented invention should expect to pay to the patent owner and that the owner should expect to receive. A reasonable royalty is the minimum amount of damages that a patent owner may recover.

NOTE

A patent owner may recover two different types of damages for patent infringement. The first, referred to as "lost profits," entitles a patent owner to recover the profits that it would have made "but for" the infringement. The second, referred to as a "reasonable royalty," entitles a patent owner to recover a royalty on the infringer's sales.

In general, when a patent owner sells the patented invention or a product that directly competes with the infringing product, the patent owner is entitled to the profits it lost as a result of the infringement. It is the patent owner's burden to prove that "but for" the infringement, the patent owner would have made the sales made by the infringer. One way in which a patent owner can prove entitlement to lost profits is by satisfying the oft-cited *Panduit* test, which requires that the patent owner establish: (1) a demand existed for the patented product; (2) there were no acceptable non-infringing substitutes; (3) the patent owner had the manufacturing and marketing capability to exploit the demand; and (4) the amount of profit the patent owner would have made. *Panduit Corp. v. Stahlin Bros. Fibre Works*, 575 F.2d 1152, 1156 (6th Cir. 1978); *see also BIC Leisure Products, Inc.* v. *Windsurfing Int'l.*, 1 F.3d 1214 (Fed. Cir. 1993); *Water Techs. Corp.* v. *Calco, Ltd.*, 850 F.2d 660, 672 (Fed. Cir. 1988).

Once a patent owner introduces sufficient evidence to satisfy the *Panduit* test, the burden shifts to the accused infringer to show that lost profits would be inappropriate for all or some of the infringing sales. *Rite-Hite Corp.* v. *Kelley, Co.*, 56 F.3d 1538, 1545 (Fed. Cir. 1995) (*en banc*).

The *Panduit* test is, however, but one of several ways in which a patent owner may prove entitlement to lost profits. *See Rite-Hite*, 56 F.3d at 1548 (emphasizing that "[i]f there are other ways to show that the infringement in fact caused the patent [owner's] lost profits, there is no reason why another test should not be acceptable"). The Federal Circuit has recognized two other tests for determining "but for" causation—the "two-supplier market" and the "market-share" tests.

Under the "two-supplier market" test, "but for" causation may be inferred when a patent owner and the accused infringer are the only suppliers in a market. *See Lam, Inc.* v. *Johns-Mansville Corp.*, 718 F.2d 1056, 1065 (Fed. Cir. 1983) ("Where, as here, the patent owner and the infringer were the only suppliers of the product, causation may be inferred."); *see also Kaufman Co.* v. *Lantech, Inc.*, 926 F.2d 1136, 1141 (Fed. Cir. 1991).

Under the "market-share" test, a patent owner may recover lost profits, even though acceptable non-infringing substitutes exist, based on the percentage of the accused infringer's sales that equal the patent owner's market share for the patented invention. *See State Indus., Inc.* v. *Mor-Flo Indus., Inc.*, 883 F.2d 1573, 1578 (Fed. Cir. 1989) (holding that the existence of non-infringing alternatives did not prohibit the patentee from obtaining lost profits for the sales it would have reasonably made based on its market share.); *see also Crystal Semiconductor Corp.* v. *Tritech Microelecs. Int'l*, 246 F.3d 1336, 1354–56 (Fed. Cir. 2001).

Even if a patent owner is not entitled to lost profits, it will nevertheless be entitled to receive a reasonable royalty on the accused infringer's sales. *Rite-Hite*, 56 F.3d at 1538; *Georgia-Pacific Corp.* v. *U.S. Plywood Corp.*, 318 F. Supp. 1116, 1120 (S.D.N.Y. 1970). The reasonable royalty analysis based on a hypothetical negotiation requires the court to envision the terms of a license agreement "reached as a result of a supposed meeting between the patent [owner] and the infringer at the time the infringement began." *Rite-Hite*, 56 F.3d at 1554. The Federal Circuit, has, however, cautioned that it is often inaccurate to characterize the negotiation as occurring between a willing licensor and licensee. *Id.* at 1554 n.13. In *Fromson* v. *Western Litho Plate & Supply Co.*, 853 F.2d 1568, 1575 (Fed. Cir. 1988), the Court emphasized that such a characterization may create the impression that "blatant, blind appropriation of inventions patented by individuals, nonmanufacturing inventors is the profitable, can't-lose course." Thus, in situations where the patent owner has shown that it was not willing to license the patented invention, it may be appropriate to award the patent owner damages based on a higher royalty rate. *Rite-Hite*, 56 F.3d at 1554–55.

AUTHORITIES

Grain Processing Corp. v. *Am. Maize-Prods. Co.*, 185 F.3d 1341, 1349 (Fed. Cir. 1999); *Tec Air, Inc.* v. *Denso Mfg. Mich., Inc.*, 192 F.3d 1353, 1362 (Fed Cir. 1999); *Fonar Corp.* v. *Gen. Elec. Co.*, 107 F.3d 1543, 1553 (Fed. Cir. 1997); *Oiness* v. *Walgreen Co.*, 88 F.3d 1025, 1029 (Fed. Cir. 1996); *Zygo Corp.* v. *Wyko Corp.*, 79 F.3d 1563, 1571 (Fed. Cir. 1996); *Rite-Hite Corp.* v. *Kelley, Co.*, 56 F.3d 1538, 1545 (Fed. Cir. 1995) (*en banc*); *BIC Leisure Products, Inc.* v. *Windsurfing Int'l.*, 1 F.3d 1214 (Fed. Cir. 1993); *SmithKline Diagnostics, Inc.* v. *Helena Labs., Corp.*, 926 F.2d 1161, 1164 (Fed. Cir. 1991); *State Indus., Inc.* v. *Mor-Flo Indus., Inc.*, 883 F.2d 1573, 1576–77 (Fed. Cir. 1989); *Water Techs. Corp.* v. *Calco, Ltd.*, 850 F.2d 660, 672 (Fed. Cir. 1988); *Panduit Corp.* v. *Stahlin Bros. Fibre Works, Inc.*, 575 F.2d 1152, 1156 (6th Cir. 1978); *Georgia-Pacific Corp.* v. *U.S. Plywood Corp.*, 318 F. Supp. 1116, 1120 (S.D.N.Y. 1970).

11.5   Lost Profits—in General

I will first instruct you about lost profit damages. Simply stated, lost profit damages are the profits [plaintiff] lost because of the infringement. They are not the profits [defendant] made.

[Plaintiff] says that it lost profits because [defendant's] infringement took away sales that [plaintiff] would have made. This is called lost profits due to lost sales.

[Plaintiff] also says that it lost profits because it had to [lower its prices or was unable to raise its prices] in order to compete with [defendant's] infringement. [Plaintiff] says that because it had to [lower its prices or was unable to raise its prices], it made less profits on the sales it made than it would have made had it not had to compete with [defendant]. This is called lost profits due to price erosion.

Finally, [plaintiff] says that its expenses increased because of [defendant's] infringement, and this lowered its profits.

[Plaintiff] has the burden to show that it was more probable than not that it would have made additional profits if [defendant] had not infringed.

Remember, if you find [plaintiff] did not prove infringement of a valid patent claim, there can be no damages of any kind.

NOTE

Include only those elements of lost profits asserted by plaintiff.

AUTHORITIES

Grain Processing Corp. v. *Am. Maize-Prods. Co.*, 185 F.3d 1341, 1349 (Fed. Cir. 1999); *Fonar Corp.* v. *Gen. Elec. Co.*, 107 F.3d 1543, 1553 (Fed. Cir. 1997); *Zygo Corp.* v. *Wyko Corp.*, 79 F.3d 1563, 1571 (Fed. Cir. 1996); *Rite-Hite Corp.* v. *Kelley, Co.*, 56 F.3d 1538, 1545 (Fed. Cir. 1995) (*en banc*); *BIC Leisure Products, Inc.* v. *Windsurfing Int'l.*, 1 F.3d 1214 (Fed. Cir. 1993); *SmithKline Diagnostics, Inc.* v. *Helena Labs., Corp.*, 926 F.2d

1161, 1164 (Fed. Cir. 1991); *State Indus., Inc. v. Mor-Flo Indus., Inc.*, 883 F.2d 1573, 1576–77 (Fed. Cir. 1989); *Water Techs. Corp. v. Calco, Ltd.*, 850 F.2d 660, 672 (Fed. Cir. 1988); *Panduit Corp. v. Stahlin Bros. Fibre Works, Inc.*, 575 F.2d 1152, 1156 (6th Cir. 1978).

11.6   Lost Profits Due to Lost Sales

Lost sales are those sales the patent owner lost because of the infringement.

To prove that it lost sales, [plaintiff] must prove that it was more probable than not that it would have made additional sales if [defendant] had not [made the sales/carried out the activities] you find to be an infringement.

[Plaintiff] may receive damages for lost sales only on those [products or processes] that compete with [defendant's] [products or processes] that you find to infringe, and that are functionally part of the competing product. [Plaintiff] may not receive lost profit damages for other products or services that might be sold along with the competing product for convenience or business advantage, but that are not functionally part of the competing product.

NOTE

Damages for lost sales are assessed based on the "entire market rule." The "entire market value" rule permits a patent owner to recover damages for infringing products/processes and for unpatented components of infringing products that are functionally related to the patented product, but not for functionally unrelated products that are sold with the infringing products. *See Rite-Hite Corp.* v. *Kelley Co.*, 56 F.3d 1538, 1550 (Fed. Cir. 1995) (*en banc*) (holding that "[o]ur precedent has not extended liability to include items that have essentially no functional relationship to the patented invention and that may have been sold with an infringing device only as a matter of convenience or business advantage"). A patent owner may also recover damages for lost sales of the patent owner's products that compete with the infringing products, even if the patent owner's product is not itself covered by the claims of the asserted patent. *King Instruments Corp.* v. *Perego*, 65 F.3d 941, 952–53 (Fed. Cir. 1995).

AUTHORITIES

Grain Processing Corp. v. *Am. Maize-Prods. Comp.*, 185 F.3d 1341, 1349 (Fed. Cir. 1999); *Tec Air, Inc.* v. *Denso Mfg. Mich.*,

Inc., 192 F.3d 1353, 1362 (Fed. Cir. 1999); *Oiness* v. *Walgreen Co.*, 88 F.3d 1025, 1029 (Fed. Cir. 1996); *King Instruments Corp.* v. *Perego*, 65 F.3d 941, 952–53 (Fed. Cir. 1995); *Rite-Hite Corp.* v. *Kelley Co.*, 56 F.3d 1538, 1550 (Fed. Cir. 1995) (*en banc*); *State Indus., Inc.* v. *Mor-Flo Indus., Inc.*, 883 F.2d 1573, 1578 (Fed. Cir. 1989); *Panduit Corp.* v. *Stahlin Bros. Fibre Works, Inc.*, 575 F.2d 1152, 1157–58 (6th Cir. 1978).

11.6.1 Manufacturing and Marketing Ability

In deciding whether [plaintiff] lost sales, you should consider whether or not [plaintiff] has proved that it had the manufacturing capacity and the marketing capability to make the sales it says it lost.

[Plaintiff] must prove that it was more probable than not that it could have made, or could have had someone else make for it, the additional products it says it could have sold but for the infringement.

[Plaintiff] also must prove that it had the capability to market and sell the additional products.

NOTE

A key factor in determining whether to award lost profits for infringing sales is manufacturing capacity. *Kearns* v. *Chrysler Corp.*, 32 F.3d 1541, 1551 (Fed. Cir. 1994). A patent owner must be able to show that it had the actual manufacturing capacity, the inventory, or the resources and business potential to increase its capacity to have made the lost sales. *See e.g. Fonar Corp.* v. *General Elec. Co.*, 107 F.3d 1543, 1553 (Fed. Cir. 1997) (evidence of fast corporate growth rate and large number of employees was sufficient to show that the plaintiff could have increased production from 8 to 500 machines per month within four years). The potential for increased capacity cannot, however, be merely "tentative, speculative and contingent." *Kearns*, 32 F.3d at 1551–52 (lost profits denied where the trial court determined that the plaintiff's evidence of manufacturing capacity was "tentative, speculative and contingent").

AUTHORITIES

Gargoyles, Inc. v. *United States*, 113 F.3d 1572, 1577–78 (Fed. Cir. 1997); *Fonar Corp.* v. *General Elec. Co.*, 107 F.3d 1543, 1553 (Fed. Cir. 1997); *Stryker Corp.* v. *Intermedics Orthopedics, Inc.*,

96 F.3d 1409, 1417–18 (Fed. Cir. 1996); *Minco, Inc.* v. *Combustion Eng'g, Inc.*, 95 F.3d 1109, 1119 (Fed. Cir. 1996); *Rite-Hite Corp.* v. *Kelley Co.*, 56 F.3d 1538, 1545 (Fed. Cir. 1995) (*en banc*); *Kearns* v. *Chrysler Corp.*, 32 F.3d 1541, 1551 (Fed. Cir. 1994).

11.6.2   Absence of Acceptable Non-infringing Substitutes

In determining whether [plaintiff] lost sales due to infringement, you must consider whether or not, if [defendant's] infringing [product or process] were not available, some or all of the people who bought from [defendant] would have bought a different, non-infringing product from [defendant] or from somebody else, rather than buy from [plaintiff]. [In that regard, you should consider a product sold by one of [plaintiff's] licensees to be a non-infringing product.]

In deciding whether or not people who bought from [defendant] would have bought a non-infringing product, you should consider whether or not there was such a demand for the patented aspects of the infringing product that purchasers would not have bought a non-infringing product.

NOTE

Non-infringing substitutes that may preclude a grant of lost profits include products on the market during the period of infringement. *Grain Processing Corp.* v. *Am. Maize-Prods. Co.*, 185 F.3d 1341, 1349 (Fed. Cir. 1999). The law remains unclear, however, whether or not a product must be on the market to be considered a non-infringing substitute. In *Zygo Corp.* v. *Wyko Corp.*, 79 F.3d 1563, 1571 (Fed. Cir. 1996), the Federal Circuit held that "[i]t is axiomatic . . . that if a device is not available for purchase, a defendant cannot argue that the device is an acceptable non-infringing alternative for the purposes of avoiding a lost profits award." The Court explained that "[a] lost profits award reflects the realities of sales actually lost, not the possibilities of a hypothetical market which the infringer might have created." *Id.*

In contrast, in *Grain Processing*, the Federal Circuit observed that a product not on the market may nevertheless be considered a non-infringing substitute. 185 F.3d 1341. The Court explained that "a fair and accurate reconstruction of the 'but for' market also must take into account, where relevant, alternative actions the infringer foreseeably would have undertaken had he not infringed." *Id.* at 1350–51. This is because "a rational would-be infringer is likely to offer an acceptable non-infringing alternative, if available, to compete with the patent owner rather than leave the market altogether." *Id.* at 1351. Thus, an accused infringer may attempt to prove that a non-infringing alternative was available, even though it was not on the market during the period of infringement. *Id.* at 1353. The Court cautioned, however, that an accused infringer's showing must amount to more than conclusory assertions because "the infringer chose to produce the infringing, rather than non-infringing product." *Id.*

AUTHORITIES

Crystal Semiconductor Corp. v. *Tritech Microelecs. Int'l, Inc.*, 246 F.3d 1336, 1356 (Fed. Cir. 2001); *Tate Access Floors, Inc.* v. *Maxcess Techs., Inc.*, 222 F.3d 958, 971 (Fed. Cir. 2000); *Grain Processing Corp.* v. *Am. Maize-Prod.*, 185 F.3d 1341, 1349 (Fed. Cir. 1999); *Gargoyles, Inc.* v. *United States*, 113 F.3d 1572, 1578–79 (Fed. Cir. 1997); *Stryker Corp.* v. *Intermedics Orthopedics, Inc.*, 96 F.3d 1409, 1417–18 (Fed. Cir. 1996); *Zygo Corp.* v. *Wyko Corp.*, 79 F.3d 1563, 1571 (Fed. Cir. 1996); *Rite-Hite Corp.* v. *Kelley Co.*, 56 F.3d 1538, 1548 (Fed. Cir. 1995) (*en banc*); *Slimfold Mfg. Co.* v. *Kinkead Indus., Inc.*, 932 F.2d 1453 (Fed. Cir. 1991); *Kaufman Co.* v. *Lantech, Inc.*, 926 F.2d 1136, 1142 (Fed. Cir. 1991); *SmithKline Diagnostics, Inc.* v. *Helena Labs., Corp.*, 926 F.2d 1161, 1164 (Fed. Cir. 1991); *State Indus., Inc.* v. *Mor-Flo Indus., Inc.*, 883 F.2d 1573, 1576-77 (Fed. Cir. 1989).

11.7   Lost Profits Due to Price Erosion/Cost Escalation

[Plaintiff] says that it also lost profits because it had to lower its prices, or was unable to raise its prices, because of [defendant's] infringement. [Plaintiff] must prove that it lowered its prices, or did not raise them, because of the infringement, and not for some other reason.

[Plaintiff] says that it also lost profits because its costs went up as a result of [defendant's] alleged infringement. [Plaintiff] must prove that it was more probable than not that its costs went up because of [defendant's] actions.

NOTE

In certain circumstances, a patent owner may be entitled to recover damages in the form of price erosion for the sales that it made during the infringement period. "To prove price erosion damages, a patent [owner] must show that, but for the infringement, it would have been able to charge higher prices." *Minco, Inc.* v. *Combustion Eng'g, Inc.*, 95 F.3d 1109, 1120 (Fed. Cir. 1996) (holding that price erosion damages were too speculative because the patented invention's sale price both increased and decreased during the infringement period); *Fiskars, Inc.* v. *Hunt Mfg. Co.*, 221 F.3d 1318, 1324–25 (Fed. Cir. 2000) (affirming district court damages award for past and future price erosion). Factors to consider in determining whether damages for price erosion are appropriate include "the nature, or definition, of the market, similarities between any benchmark market and the market in which the price erosion is alleged, and the effect of the hypothetically increased price on the likely number of sales at that price in that market." *Crystal Semiconductor Corp.* v. *Tritech Microelecs. Int'l, Inc.*, 246 F.3d 1336, 1357 (Fed. Cir. 2001).

In *Crystal Semiconductor*, the Court held that the patent owner was not entitled to price erosion damages, based in part on the patent owner's failure to show the impact of a price increase on the sales it made and would have made. *Id.* at 1359. The Court explained that "the patent [owner] cannot show entitlement to a higher price divorced from the effect of that higher price on demand for the product." *Id.* at 1357.

AUTHORITIES

Crystal Semiconductor Corp. v. *Tritech Microelecs. Int'l, Inc.*, 246 F.3d 1336, 1357–60 (Fed. Cir. 2001); *Fiskars, Inc.* v. *Hunt Mfg. Co.*, 221 F.3d 1318, 1324–25 (Fed. Cir. 2000); *Minco, Inc.* v. *Combustion Eng'g, Inc.*, 95 F.3d 1109, 1120 (Fed. Cir. 1996).

11.8   Amount of Lost Profits

If [plaintiff] has proved that it lost profits due to infringement by [defendant], then you are to determine the amount of profits that [plaintiff] lost. [Plaintiff] must prove the amount of its lost profits to a reasonable probability. That is, the amount of lost profits damages should not include amounts that are merely speculative. However, if the reason that [plaintiff] has difficulty proving the amount of its lost profits is because [defendant] did not keep records or destroyed records, such as records of its sales, then you should resolve doubts as to the amount against [defendant].

AUTHORITIES

Tate Access Floors, Inc. v. *Maxcess Techs., Inc.*, 222 F.3d 958, 971 (Fed. Cir. 2000); *Grain Processing Corp.* v. *Am. Maize-Prods. Co.*, 185 F.3d 1341, 1349–50 (Fed. Cir. 1999); *Gargoyles, Inc.* v. *United States*, 113 F.3d 1572, 1574–77 (Fed. Cir. 1997); *Oiness* v. *Walgreen Co.*, 88 F.3d 1025, 1029–32 (Fed. Cir. 1996).

11.9   Reasonable Royalty

[Plaintiff] is [also] asking for damages in the amount of a reasonable royalty [as an alternative to lost profits]. [If you find that [plaintiff] has proved lost profits for all of [defendant's] infringing [sales or activities], then the damages award to [plaintiff] should be those lost profits.]

If you find that [plaintiff] has not proved that it should recover lost profits, or that it has only proved lost profits for some of [defendant's] infringing [sales or activities], then for those infringing [sales or activities] for which you do not award lost profits, you should determine the amount [plaintiff] has proved to be a reasonable royalty.

NOTE

Courts have held that it is within the trial court's discretion to award a royalty based on either an infringer's profits or a patentee's lost profits. *Rite-Hite Corp.* v. *Kelley Co.*, 56 F.3d 1538, 1555 (Fed. Cir. 1995) (*en banc*). For example, in *Rite-Hite* the Court rejected defendant's argument that a reasonable royalty must be based on an infringer's profits. *Id.; see also State Indus., Inc.* v. *Mor-Flo Indus., Inc.*, 883 F.2d 1573, 1580 (Fed. Cir. 1989) (holding that there is no rule that a royalty may be no higher than an infringer's profits).

AUTHORITIES

Crystal Semiconductor Corp. v. *Tritech Microelecs. Int'l, Inc.*, 246 F.3d 1336, 1357–60 (Fed. Cir. 2001); *Mahurkar* v. *C.R. Bard, Inc.*, 79 F.3d 1572, 1579 (Fed. Cir. 1996); *Minco, Inc.* v. *Combustion Eng'g, Inc.*, 95 F.3d 1109, 1119–20 (Fed. Cir. 1996); *Rite-Hite Corp.* v. *Kelley Co.*, 56 F.3d 1538, 1554 (Fed. Cir. 1995) (*en banc*); *State Indus., Inc.* v. *Mor-Flo Indus., Inc.*, 883 F.2d 1573, 1580 (Fed. Cir. 1989).

11.9.1   What Is a Reasonable Royalty?

A royalty is an amount of money that someone pays a patent owner to be able to use the patented invention.

A reasonable royalty is the royalty that would be reasonable for the infringer to pay and for the patent owner to accept for use of a patent that they both know is valid and that the infringer wants to use.

You are to decide what a reasonable royalty would be based on circumstances as of the time just before [defendant] began [selling or using] the infringing [product or process]. You should assume that [defendant] and [plaintiff] knew at that time such things as the level of sales and profits that [defendant] would make using the invention. You should also assume that [plaintiff] was willing to grant [defendant] a license to [sell or use] the patented invention and that [defendant] was willing to pay for that license.

In deciding what is a reasonable royalty, you may consider the factors that [plaintiff] and [defendant] would consider in setting the amount [defendant] should pay.

I will list for you a number of factors you may consider. This is not every possible factor, but it will give you an idea of the kinds of things to consider in setting a reasonable royalty.

1. Whether the patent owner had established a royalty for the patented invention, for example, by granting other licenses at that royalty. You should remember, however, that an established royalty may have been set before the patent was determined to be valid and infringed in court and, therefore, may not be as much as it would be if both the patent owner and the party wanting to use the patent know it is valid.

2. Royalties paid by [defendant] or by others for patents comparable to the _____ patent.

3. Whether or not [plaintiff] had a policy of licensing or not licensing the patent.

4. Whether or not [plaintiff] and [defendant] are competitors.

5. Whether being able to use the patented invention helps in making sales of other products or services.

6. The profitability of the product made using the patent, and whether or not it is commercially successful or popular.

7. The advantages and benefits of using the patented invention over [products or processes] not claimed in the _____ patent.

8. The extent of [defendant's] use of the patented invention and the value of that use to [defendant].

9. Whether or not there is a portion or percentage of the profit or selling price that is customarily paid in [identify field] for use of patented inventions comparable to the inventions claimed in the _____ patent.

10. The portion of the profit that is due to the patented invention, as compared to the portion of the profit due to other factors, such as unpatented elements or unpatented manufacturing processes, or features or improvements developed by [defendant].

11. Expert opinions as to what would be a reasonable royalty.

AUTHORITIES

Tec Air, Inc. v. *Denso Mfg. Mich., Inc.*, 192 F.3d 1353, 1362 (Fed. Cir. 1999); *Fonar Corp.* v. *Gen. Elec. Co.*, 107 F.3d 1543, 1552–53 (Fed. Cir. 1997); *Mahurkar* v. *C.R. Bard, Inc.*, 79 F.3d 1572, 1579–81 (Fed. Cir. 1996); *Maxwell* v. *J. Baker, Inc.*, 86 F.3d 1098, 1108–10 (Fed. Cir. 1996); *Rite-Hite Corp.* v. *Kelley Co.*, 56 F.3d 1538, 1554 (Fed. Cir. 1995) (*en banc*); *Georgia-Pacific Corp.* v. *United States Plywood Corp.*, 318 F. Supp. 1116, 1120 (S.D.N.Y. 1970).

11.10   Total Damages

After making your findings concerning lost profits damages and reasonable royalty damages, you should arrive at a total damages amount to award to [plaintiff]. This amount should include the amount of lost profits damages [plaintiff] has proved. It also should include the reasonable royalty damages for that portion of the infringement for which [plaintiff] did not prove lost profits damages.

NOTE

Use this instruction when a mixed measure of damages is sought.

Table of Cases

Bayer AG v. Elan Pharm. Research Corp., 212 F.3d 1241 (Fed. Cir. 2000), **7.3, 7.4**

Bayer AG v. Schein Pharma., Inc., 301 F.3d 1306 (Fed. Cir. 2002), **9.1.3**

BBA Nonwovens Simpsonville, Inc. v. Superior Nonwovens, LLC, 303 F.3d 1322 (Fed. Cir. 2002), **6.4**

Bell Atlantic Network Servs., Inc. v. Covad Communications Group, Inc., 262 F.3d 1258 (Fed. Cir. 2001), **6.1, 7.4**

Bey v. Kollonitsch, 806 F.2d 1024 (Fed. Cir. 1986), **9.3.1, 9.3.9**

BIC Leisure Products, Inc. v. Windsurfing Int'l., 1 F.3d 1214 (Fed. Cir. 1993), **11.4, 11.5**

Biovail Corp. Int'l v. Andrx Pharms., Inc., 239 F.3d 1297 (Fed. Cir. 2001), **7.3, 7.4**

Brasseler, U.S.A.I, L.P. v. Stryker Sales Corp., 182 F.3d 888 (Fed. Cir. 1999), **9.3.6**

Brown & Williamson Tobacco Corp. v. Philip Morris Inc., 229 F.3d 1120 (Fed. Cir. 2000), **9.8, 9.8.3, 9.8.4**

Bruning v. Hirose, 161 F.3d 681 (Fed. Cir. 1998), **9.3.1, 9.3.9**

Budde v. Harley-Davidson, Inc., 250 F.3d 1369 (Fed. Cir. 2001), **9.1.4**

Burroughs Wellcome Co. v. Barr Labs., 40 F.3d 1223 (Fed. Cir. 1994), **9.3.1**

Carborundum Co. v. Molten Metal Equip. Innovations, Inc., 72 F.3d 872 (Fed. Cir. 1995), **7.12.1, 7.12.2**

Carroll Touch, Inc. v. Electro Mech. Sys., Inc., 15 F.3d 1573 (Fed. Cir. 1993), **6.2**

Caterpillar Inc. v. Deere & Co., 224 F.3d 1374 (Fed. Cir. 2000), **7.5, 7.6**

Checkpoint Sys. v. United States Int'l Trade Comm'n, 54 F.3d 756 (Fed. Cir. 1995), **9.3.9**

Chiuminatta Concrete Concepts, Inc. v. Cardinal Indus., Inc., 145 F.3d 1303 (Fed. Cir. 1998), **6.4, 7.5, 7.6, 7.12.1**

Cole v. Kimberly-Clark Corp., 102 F.3d 524 (Fed. Cir. 1996), **7.4**

Comark Communications, Inc. v. Harris Corp., 156 F.3d 1182 (Fed. Cir. 1998), **8**

Constant v. Advanced Micro-Devices, Inc., 848 F.2d 1560 (Fed. Cir. 1988), **9.3.8**

Continental Plastic Containers v. Owens Brockway Plastic Prods., Inc., 141 F.3d 1073 (Fed. Cir. 1998), **9.3.6, 9.3.7**

Cooper Cameron Corp. v. Kvaerner Oilfield Prod., 291 F.3d 1317 (Fed. Cir. 2002), **9.1.1**

Cooper v. Goldfarb, 154 F.3d 1321 (Fed. Cir. 1998), **9.3.1, 9.3.9**

C.R. Bard, Inc. v. Advanced Cardiovascular Sys., Inc., 911 F.2d 670 (Fed. Cir. 1990), **7.12.2**

C.R. Bard, Inc. v. M3 Sys., Inc., 157 F.3d 1340 (Fed. Cir. 1998), **9.6**

Creo Prod. v. Presstek, Inc., 305 F.3d 1337 (Fed. Cir. 2002), **9.1.4**

Critikon, Inc. v. Becton Dickinson Vascular Access, Inc., 120 F.3d 1253 (Fed. Cir. 1997), **8, 10, 10.1, 10.2, 10.3, 10.4**

Crystal Semiconductor Corp. v. Tritech Microelecs. Int'l, Inc., 246 F.3d 1336 (Fed. Cir. 2001), **6.5, 11.3, 11.4, 11.6.2, 11.7, 11.9**

Curtis Mfg. Co. v. Plasti-Clip Corp., 888 F. Supp. 1212 (D.N.H. 1994), **7.12.1**

CVI/Beta Ventures, Inc. v. Tura LP, 905 F. Supp. 1171 (E.D.N.Y. 1999), *rev'd in part, vacated in part,* 112 F.3d 1146 (Fed Cir. 1997), **7.12.1**

Cybor Corp. v. FAS Techs., Inc., 138 F.3d 1448 (Fed. Cir. 1998), **6.1**

Dayco Products, Inc. v. Total Containment, Inc., 329 F.3d 1358 (Fed. Cir. 2003), **10.2**

Dekalb Genetics Corp. v. Northrup King Co., No. 96C 501169, 1997 WL 587492 (N.D. Ill. Aug. 14, 1997), **7.9**

DeMarini Sports, Inc. v. Worth, Inc., 239 F.3d 1314 (Fed. Cir. 2001), **7.1, 7.3**

Devices for Med., Inc. v. Boehl, 822 F.2d 1062 (Fed. Cir. 1987), **11.3**

D.L. Auld Co. v. Chroma Graphics Corp., 714 F.2d 1144 (Fed. Cir. 1983), **9.3.6**

DMI, Inc. v. Deere & Co., 802 F.2d 421 (Fed. Cir. 1986), **9**

Dow Chem. Co. v. Astro-Valcour, Inc., 267 F.3d 1334 (Fed. Cir. 2001), **9.3.9**

Dow Chem. Co. v. United States, 226 F.3d 1334 (Fed. Cir. 2000), **6.2**

Dunlop Holdings Ltd. v. Ram Golf Corp., 524 F.2d 33 (7th Cir. 1975), **9.3.9**

Durel Corp. v. Osram Sylvania, Inc., 256 F.3d 1298 (2001), **9.1.2**

Ecolochem, Inc. v. Southern Cal. Edison Co., 227 F.3d 1361 (Fed. Cir. 2000), **9.6, 9.7, 9.8, 9.8.2**

Eiselstein v. Frank, 52 F.3d 1035 (Fed. Cir. 1995), **9.1.4**

Ekchian v. Home Depot, Inc., 104 F.3d 1299 (Fed. Cir. 1997), **7.4**

Eli Lilly & Co. v. Barr Labs., Inc., 222 F.3d 973 (Fed. Cir. 2000), **9.1.3**

Elkay Mfg. Co. v. Ebco Mfg. Co., 192 F.3d 973 (Fed. Cir. 1999), **6.5.1**

Elk Corp. of Dallas v. GAF Bldg. Materials Corp., 168 F.3d 28 (Fed. Cir. 1999), **10.2**

Embrex, Inc. v. Service Eng'g Corp., 216 F.3d 1343 (Fed. Cir. 2000), **7.8**

Enzo Biochem, Inc. v. Calgene, Inc., 188 F.3d 1362 (Fed. Cir. 1999), **9, 9.1, 9.1.2**

Enzo Biochem, Inc. v. Gen-Probe, Inc., 285 F.3d 1013 (Fed. Cir. 2002), **9.1.1**

Estee Lauder Inc. v. L'Oreal, S.A., 129 F.3d 588 (Fed. Cir. 1997), **9.3.1, 9.3.9**

Evans Cooling Sys., Inc. v. General Motors Corp., 125 F.3d 1448 (Fed. Cir. 1997), **9.3.4**

Exxon Chem. Patents, Inc. v. Lubrizol Corp., 64 F.3d 1553 (Fed. Cir. 1995), **6.3, 7.9**

EZ Dock, Inc. v. Schafer Sys., Inc., 276 F.3d 1347 (Fed. Cir. 2002), **9.3.7**

Festo Corp. v. Shoketsu Kinzoku Kogyo Kabushiki Co., 234 F.3d 558 (Fed. Cir. 2000) *(en banc), vacated,* 535 U.S. 722. 122 S.Ct. 1831 (2002), *after remand,* 344 F.3d 1359 (Fed. Cir. 2003), **7.4**

Finnegan Corp. v. International Trade Comm'n, 180 F.3d 1354 (Fed. Cir. 1999), **7.10, 9.5, 9.6**

Fiskars, Inc. v. Hunt Mfg. Co., 221 F.3d 1318 (Fed. Cir. 2000), **11.7**

Florida Prepaid Postsecondary Educ. Expense Bd. v. College Sav. Bank, 527 U.S. 627 (1999), **7.1**

FMC Corp. v. Manitowoc Co., 835 F.2d 1411 (Fed. Cir. 1987), **10.4**

FMC Corp. v. Up-Right, Inc., 21 F.3d 1073 (Fed. Cir. 1994), **7.12.2**

Fonar Corp. v. General Elec. Co., 107 F.3d 1543 (Fed. Cir. 1997), **11.4, 11.5, 11.6.1, 11.9.1**

Forest Labs. v. Abbott Labs., 239 F.3d 1305 (Fed. Cir. 2001), **7.4**

Fromson v. Western Litho Plate & Supply Co., 853 F.2d 1568 (Fed. Cir. 1988), **8, 11.4**

Gambro Lundia AB v. Baxter Healthcare Corp., 110 F.3d 1573 (Fed. Cir. 1997), **9.4**

Gargoyles, Inc. v. United States, 113 F.3d 1572 (Fed. Cir. 1997), **11.6.1, 11.6.2, 11.8**

Gart v. Logitech, Inc., 254 F.3d 1334 (Fed. Cir. 2001), **11.3**

Genentech Inc. v. Chiron Corp., 220 F.3d 1345 (Fed. Cir. 2000), **9.3.1, 9.3.9**

Gentry Gallery, Inc. v. Berkline Corp., 134 F.3d 1473 (Fed. Cir. 1998), **7.4, 9.1.1**

Georgia-Pacific Corp. v. United States Gypsum Co., 195 F.3d 1322 (Fed. Cir. 1999), **6.5.1, 6.5.3, 8**

Georgia-Pacific Corp. v. U.S. Plywood Corp., 318 F. Supp. 1116 (S.D.N.Y. 1970), **11.4, 11.9.1**

Glaxo Inc. v. Novopharm Ltd., 52 F.3d 1043 (Fed. Cir. 1995), **9.1.3**

Globetrotter Software, Inc. v. Elan Computer Group, Inc., 236 F.3d 1363 (Fed. Cir. 2001), **6.2**

Gould v. Schawlow, 363 F.2d 908 (C.C.P.A. 1966), **9.3.9**

Graco, Inc. v. Binks Mfg. Co., 60 F.3d 785 (Fed. Cir. 1995), **8**

Graham v. John Deere Co., 383 U.S. 1 (1966), **9.7, 9.8, 9.8.1, 9.8.2, 9.8.3, 9.8.4**

Grain Processing Corp. v. American Maize-Prods. Co., 185 F.3d 1341 (Fed. Cir. 1999), **11.2, 11.4, 11.5, 11.6, 11.6.2, 11.8**

Graver Tank & Mfg. Co. v. Linde Air Prods. Co., 339 U.S. 605 (1950), **7.3**

Griffith v. Kanamaru, 816 F.2d 624 (Fed. Cir. 1987), **9.3.1, 9.3.9**

Group One, Ltd. v. Hallmark Cards, Inc., 254 F.3d 1041 (Fed. Cir. 2001), **9.3.6**

Hanson v. Alpine Valley Ski Area, Inc., 718 F.2d 1075 (Fed. Cir. 1983), **11.3**

Hebert v. Lisle Corp., 99 F.3d 1109 (Fed. Cir. 1996), **10**

Hewlett-Packard Co. v. Bausch & Lomb Inc., 909 F.2d 1464 (Fed. Cir. 1990), **7.12.1, 7.12.2**

Hewlett-Packard Co. v. Repeat-O-Type Stencil Mfg. Corp., 123 F.3d 1445 (Fed. Cir. 1997), **6.5**

Hill-Rom Co. v. Kinetic Concepts, Inc., 209 F.3d 1337 (Fed. Cir. 2000), **6.1**

Hodosh v. Block Drug Co., 833 F.2d 1575 (Fed. Cir. 1987), **7.12.2**

Hoechst Celanese Corp. v. BP Chems. Ltd., 78 F.3d 1575 (Fed. Cir. 1996), **7.11**

Hyatt v. Boone, 146 F.3d 1348 (Fed. Cir. 1998), **9.3.1, 9.3.9**

Hybritech Inc. v. Monoclonal Antibodies, Inc., 802 F.3d 1367 (Fed. Cir. 1986), **9.1**

IMS Tech., Inc. v. Haas Automation, Inc., 206 F.3d 1422 (Fed. Cir. 2000), **6.4, 7.5, 7.6**

Innovative Scuba Concepts, Inc. v. Feder Indus., Inc., 26 F.3d 1112 (Fed. Cir. 1994), **9.3.9**

In re Bartfeld, 925 F.2d 1450 (Fed. Cir. 1991), **9.3.10**

In re Chu, 66 F.3d 292 (Fed. Cir. 1995), **9.3.10**

In re Cronyn, 890 F.2d 1158 (Fed. Cir. 1989), **9.3.8**

In re Cruciferous Sprout Litig., 301 F.3d 1343 (Fed. Cir. 2002), **9.6**

In re Dance, 160 F.3d 1339 (Fed. Cir. 1998), **9.8.3, 9.8.4**

In re Dembiczak, 175 F.3d 994 (Fed. Cir. 1999), **9.8, 9.8.1, 9.8.2, 9.8.3**

In re Deuel, 51 F.3d 1552 (Fed. Cir. 1995), **9.8**

In re Donaldson Co., 16 F.3d 1189 (Fed. Cir. 1994), **9.1.4**

In re Dossel, 115 F.3d 942 (Fed. Cir. 1997), **9.1.4**

In re Hall, 781 F.2d 897 (Fed. Cir. 1986), **9.3.8**

In re Kotzab, 217 F.3d 1365 (Fed. Cir. 2000), **9.8, 9.8.1, 9.8.2**

In re Oelrich, 666 F.2d 578 (CCPA 1981), **9.5**

In re Paulsen, 30 F.3d 1475 (Fed. Cir. 1994), **9.5**

In re Robertson, 169 F.3d 743 (Fed. Cir. 1999), **9.3.10**

In re Rouffet, 149 F.3d 1350 (Fed. Cir. 1998), **9.8, 9.8.1**

In re Thorpe, 777 F.2d 695 (Fed. Cir. 1985), **7.9**

In re Wands, 858 F.2d 731 (Fed. Cir. 1988), **9.1**

In re Wyer, 655 F.2d 221 (C.C.P.A. 1981), **9.3.8**

Insituform Techs., Inc. v. Cat Contracting, Inc., 161 F.3d 688 (Fed. Cir. 1998), **7.12.1**

Intel Corp. v. United States Int'l Trade Comm'n, 946 F.2d 821 (Fed. Cir. 1991), **7.1**

Interactive Gift Express, Inc. v. CompuServe, Inc., 256 F.3d 1323 (Fed. Cir. 2001), **6.1**

J&M Corp. v. Harley-Davidson, Inc., 269 F.3d 1360 (Fed. Cir. 2001), **7.5**

Jeneric/Pentron, Inc. v. Dillon Co., 205 F.3d 1377 (Fed. Cir. 2000), **7.10**

Johns Hopkins Univ. v. Cellpro, 34 USPQ2d 1276 (D. Del. 1995), **8, 11**

Johnson & Johnston Assocs. v. R.E. Service Co., 238 F.3d 1347 (Fed. Cir. 2001), **7.4**

Johnson & Johnston Assocs. v. R.E. Service Co., 285 F.3d 1046 (Fed. Cir. 2002) *(en banc)*, **7.4**

Johnson Worldwide Assocs., Inc. v. Zebco Corp., 175 F.3d 985 (Fed. Cir. 1999), **6.1**

Joy Techs., Inc. v. Flakt, Inc., 6 F.3d 770 (Fed. Cir. 1993), **7.12.1, 7.12.2**

Juicy Whip, Inc. v. Orange Bang, Inc., 292 F.3d 728 (Fed. Cir. 2002), **10, 10.1**

KangaROOS U.S.A., Inc. v. Caldor, Inc., 778 F.2d 1571 (Fed. Cir. 1985), **10.1**

Kaufman Co. v. Lantech, Inc., 926 F.2d 1136 (Fed. Cir. 1991), **11.4, 11.6.2**

Kearns v. Chrysler Corp., 32 F.3d 1541 (Fed. Cir. 1994), **11.6.1**

Kimberly-Clark Corp.v. Johnson & Johnson, 745 F.2d 1437 (Fed. Cir. 1984), **9.2**

King Instruments Corp. v. Perego, 65 F.3d 941 (Fed. Cir. 1995), **11.6**

Kingsdown Med. Consultants, Ltd. v. Hollister, Inc., 863 F.2d 867 (Fed. Cir. 1988) *(en banc)*, **10.1, 10.3**

Kloster Speedsteel AB v. Crucible Inc., 793 F.2d 1565 (Fed. Cir. 1986), **8**

Knorr-Bremse Systeme Fuer Nutzfahrzeuge GmbH v. Dana Corp., 2004 U.S. App. LEXIS 19185 (Fed. Cir. Sept. 13, 2004), **8**

K-2 Corp. v. Salomon S.A., 191 F.3d 1356 (Fed. Cir. 1999), **7.4**

Lam, Inc. v. Johns-Manville Corp., 718 F.2d 1056 (Fed. Cir. 1983), **11.4**

Lamb-Weston, Inc. v. McCain Foods, Ltd., 78 F.3d 540 (Fed. Cir. 1996), **9.3.3, 9.3.10, 9.4**

Lampi Corp. v. American Power Prods., Inc., 228 F.3d 1365 (Fed. Cir. 2000), **9.1.1**

Lans v. Digital Equip. Corp., 252 F.3d 1320 (Fed. Cir. 2001), **11.3**

Lewmar Marine, Inc. v. Barient, Inc., 827 F.2d 744 (Fed. Cir. 1987), **9.5**

Life Tech., Inc. v. Clontech Labs., Inc., 224 F.3d 1320 (Fed. Cir. 2000), **10.2**

Li Second Family Ltd. P'ship v. Toshiba Corp., 231 F.3d 1373 (Fed. Cir. 2000), **10, 10.2, 10.3, 10.4**

Litton Sys., Inc. v. Honeywell, Inc., 87 F.3d 1559 (Fed. Cir. 1996), *appeal after remand*, 238 F.3d 1376 (Fed. Cir. 2001), **7.4, 10.2**

LNP Eng'g Plastics, Inc. v. Miller Waste Mills, Inc., 275 F.3d 1347 (Fed. Cir. 2001), **9.1.4, 9.8**

Lockwood v. American. Airlines, Inc., 107 F.3d 1565 (Fed. Cir. 1997), **9.1, 9.1.1, 9.3.3, 9.3.5**

Loctite Corp. v. Ultraseal Ltd., 781 F.2d 861 (Fed. Cir. 1985), **7.1**

Loral Fairchild, Corp. v. Victor Co. of Japan, Ltd., 906 F. Supp. 813 (E.D.N.Y. 1995), **11.3**

Lough v. Brunswick Corp., 86 F.3d 1113 (Fed. Cir. 1996), *reh'g en banc denied*, 103 F.3d 1517 (Fed. Cir. 1997), **9.3.4, 9.3.7**

Madey v. Duke Univ., 307 F.3d 1351 (Fed. Cir. 2002), **9.3.7**

Mahurkar v. C.R. Bard, Inc., 79 F.3d 1572 (Fed. Cir. 1996), **9.3.1, 9.3.8, 9.3.9, 11.9, 11.9.1**

Mannesmann Demag Corp. v. Engineered Metal Prods. Co., 793 F.2d 1279 (Fed. Cir. 1986), **6.5.3**

Manville Sales Corp. v. Paramount Sys., Inc., 917 F.2d 544 (Fed. Cir. 1990), **7.12.1, 7.12.2**

Markman v. Westview Instruments, Inc., 52 F.3d 967 (Fed. Cir. 1995) *(en banc)*, *aff'd*, 517 U.S. 370 (1995), **6.1, 7**

Marsh-McBirney, Inc. v. Montedoro-Whitney Corp., 882 F.2d 498 (Fed. Cir. 1989), **6.2, 7.11**

Masco Corp. v. United States, 303 F.3d 1316 (Fed. Cir. 2002), **6.4**

Massachusetts Inst. of Tech. v. AB Fortia, 774 F.2d 1104 (Fed. Cir. 1985), **9.3.8**

Maxwell v. J. Baker, Inc., 86 F.3d 1098 (Fed. Cir. 1996), **7.4, 11.2, 11.3, 11.9.1**

McGinley v. Franklin Sports, Inc., 262 F.3d 1339 (Fed. Cir. 2001), **9.7**

Medtronic, Inc. v. Advanced Cardiovascular Sys., Inc., 248 F.3d 1303 (Fed. Cir. 2001), **7.5**

Mehl/Biophile Int'l Corp. v. Milgraum, 192 F.3d 1362 (Fed. Cir. 1999), **9.5**

Mentor Corp. v. Colopast, Inc., 998 F.2d 992 (Fed. Cir. 1993), **6.3, 7.9**

Mentor H/S, Inc. v. Medical Device Alliance, Inc., 244 F.3d 1365 (Fed. Cir. 2001), **9.1, 9.1.3**

Micro Chem., Inc. v. Great Plains Chem. Co., 194 F.3d 1250 (Fed. Cir. 1999), **7.12.1**

Minco, Inc. v. Combustion Eng'g, Inc., 95 F.3d 1109 (Fed. Cir. 1996), **11.6.1, 11.7, 11.9**

Minnesota Mining & Mfg. v. Johnson and Johnson Orthopedics, Inc., 976 F.2d 1559 (Fed. Cir. 1992), **8**

Minuteman Int'l, Inc. v. Critical-Vac Filtration Corp., No. 95C 7255, 1997 WL 187326 (N.D. Ill. April 11, 1997), **6.1**

Mitsubishi Elec. Corp. v. Ampex Corp., 190 F. 3d 1300 (Fed. Cir. 1999), **9.3.4**

Moba, B.V. v. Diamond Automation, Inc., 325 F.3d 1306 (Fed. Cir. 2003), **7.12.1**

Molins PLC v. Textron, Inc., 48 F.3d 1172 (Fed. Cir. 1995), **10, 10.2, 10.3, 10.4**

Monarch Knitting Mach. Corp. v. Sulzer Morat GmbH, 139 F.3d 877 (Fed. Cir. 1998), **9.8.1, 9.8.2**

Monon Corp. v. Stoughton Trailers, Inc., 239 F.3d 1253 (Fed. Cir. 2001), **9.3.6, 9.3.7**

Moore U.S.A., Inc. v. Standard Register Co., 229 F.3d 1091 (Fed. Cir. 2000), **7.3, 7.4**

Morgan v. Hirsch, 728 F.2d 1449 (Fed. Cir. 1984), **9.3.1**

Mycogen Plant Sci., Inc. v. Monsanto Co., 243 F.3d 1316 (Fed. Cir. 2001), **9.3.1, 9.3.9**

Mycogen Plant Sci., Inc. v. Monsanto Co., 252 F.3d 1306 (Fed. Cir. 2001), **7.4**

National Presto Indus., Inc. v. West Bend Co., 76 F.3d 1185 (Fed. Cir. 1996), **7.11, 8**

National Recovery Techs., Inc. v. Magnetic Separation Sys., Inc., 166 F.3d 1190 (Fed. Cir. 1999), **9.1, 9.1.2**

New Railhead Mfg., L.L.C. v. Vermeer Mfg. Co., 298 F.3d 1290 (Fed. Cir. 2002), **9.3.7**

Nike Inc. v. Wal-Mart Stores, 138 F.3d 1437 (Fed. Cir. 1998), **11.3**

North Am. Vaccine, Inc. v. American Cynamid Co., 7 F.3d 1571 (Fed. Cir. 1993), **9.1.4**

Northern Telecom, Inc. v. Datapoint Corp., 908 F.2d 931 (Fed. Cir. 1990), **9.3.8, 10.1**

Northern Telecom Ltd. v. Samsung Elecs. Co., 215 F.3d 1281 (Fed. Cir. 2000), **9.1, 9.1.3**

Nyko Mfg. Co. v. Nu-Star, Inc., 950 F.2d 714 (Fed. Cir. 1991), **9.8.2**

Oddzon Prods., Inc. v. Just Toys, Inc., 122 F.3d 1396 (Fed. Cir. 1997), **9.4**

Odetics, Inc. v. Storage Tech. Corp., 185 F.3d 1259 (Fed. Cir. 1999), **6.4, 7.5, 7.6**

Oiness v. Walgreen Co., 88 F.3d 1025 (Fed. Cir. 1996), **11.4, 11.6, 11.8**

Orthokinetics, Inc. v. Safety Travel Chairs, Inc., 806 F.2d 1565 (Fed. Cir. 1986), **9.8**

Ortho Pharm. Corp. v. Smith, 959 F.2d 936 (Fed. Cir. 1992), **8**

Pall Corp. v. Micron Separations, Inc., 66 F.3d 1211 (Fed. Cir. 1995), **9.1.4, 11, 11.2**

Palmer v. Dudzik, 481 F.2d 1377 (C.C.P.A. 1973), **9.3.9**

Panduit Corp. v. Stahlin Bros. Fibre Works, Inc., 575 F.2d 1152 (6th Cir. 1978), **11.4, 11.5, 11.6**

Pannu v. Iolab Corp., 155 F.3d 1344 (Fed. Cir. 1998), **9.4**

Payless Shoesource, Inc. v. Reebok Int'l Ltd., 998 F.2d 985 (Fed. Cir. 1993), **7.1**

Pennwalt Corp. v. Durand-Wayland, Inc., 833 F.2d 931 (Fed. Cir. 1987) *(en banc)*, **7.3**

PerSeptive Biosystems, Inc. v. Pharmacia Biotech, Inc., 225 F.3d 1315 (Fed. Cir. 2000), **10, 10.1, 10.2, 10.3**

Personalized Media Communications, L.L.C. v. International Trade Comm'n, 161 F.3d 696 (Fed. Cir. 1998), **9.1, 9.1.4**

Pfaff v. Wells Elecs., Inc., 525 U.S. 55 (1998), **9.3.6**

Phillips Petroleum Co. v. Huntsman Polymers Corp., 157 F.3d 866 (Fed. Cir. 1998), **6.5.1**

PIN/NIP, Inc. v. Platte Chem. Co., 304 F.3d 1235 (Fed. Cir. 2002), **9.1.1**

Pioneer Magnetics, Inc. v. Micro Linear Corp., 238 F.3d 1341 (Fed. Cir. 2001), *after remand*, 330 F.3d 1352 (Fed. Cir. 2003), **7.4**

Pitney Bowes, Inc. v. Hewlett-Packard Co., 182 F.3d 1298 (Fed. Cir. 1999), **6.1**

Porter v. Farmers Supply Serv., Inc., 790 F.2d 882 (Fed. Cir. 1986), **7.12**

PPG Indus. v. Guardian Indus. Corp., 156 F.3d 1351 (Fed. Cir. 1998), **6.5.2**

Preemption Devices, Inc. v. Minnesota Mining & Mfg. Co., 803 F.2d 1170 (Fed. Cir. 1986), **7.12.2**

Price v. Symsek, 988 F.2d 1187 (Fed. Cir. 1993), **9.4**

Purdue Pharma L.P. v. F.H. Faulding & Co., 48 F. Supp. 2d 420 (D. Del. 1999), *aff'd*, 230 F.3d 1320 (Fed. Cir. 2000), **9.1.1**

Read Corp. v. Portec, Inc., 970 F.2d 816 (Fed. Cir. 1992), **8**

Refac Int'l, Ltd. v. Lotus Dev. Corp., 81 F.3d 1576 (Fed. Cir. 1996), **10, 10.3**

Reiffin v. Microsoft Corp., 214 F.3d 1342 (Fed. Cir. 2000), **9.1.1**

Riles v. Shell Exploration and Prod. Co., 298 F.3d 1302 (Fed. Cir. 2002), **7.3**

Rite-Hite Corp. v. Kelley Co., 56 F.3d 1538 (Fed. Cir. 1995) *(en banc)*, **11, 11.2, 11.4, 11.5, 11.6, 11.6.1, 11.6.2, 11.9, 11.9.1**

Rival Co. v. Sunbeam Corp., 987 F. Supp. 1167 (W.D. Miss. 1997), *aff'd without op.*, 185 F.3d 885 (Fed. Cir. 1999), **6.1**

Robotic Vision Sys., Inc. v. View Eng'g, Inc., 249 F.3d 1307 (Fed. Cir. 2001), **9.3.6**

Roche Prods., Inc. v. Bolar Pharm. Co., 733 F.2d 858 (Fed. Cir. 1984), **7.8**

Rosco, Inc. v. Mirror Lite Co., 304 F.3d 1373 (Fed. Cir. 2002), **7.2**

Ruiz v. A.B. Chance Co., 234 F.3d 654 (Fed. Cir. 2000), **9.7, 9.8, 9.8.1, 9.8.2, 9.8.3, 9.8.4**

Ryko Mfg. Co. v. Nu-Star, Inc., 950 F.2d 714 (Fed. Cir. 1991), **9.8.1, 9.8.3, 9.8.4**

Sage Prods., Inc. v. Devon Indus., Inc., 45 F.3d 1575 (Fed. Cir. 1995), **7.12.2**

Sage Prods., Inc. v. Devon Indus., Inc., 126 F.3d 1420 (Fed. Cir. 1997), **7.4**

Scaltech, Inc. v. Retech/Tetra, LLC, 269 F.3d 1321 (Fed. Cir. 2001), **9.3.6**

Schwing GMBH v. Putzmeister Aktiengesellschaft, 305 F.3d 1318 (Fed. Cir. 2002), **7.4**

SciMed Life Sys., Inc. v. Advanced Cardiovascular Sys., 242 F.3d 1337 (Fed. Cir. 2001), **6.1**

Scripps Clinic & Research Found. v. Genentech, Inc., 927 F.2d 1565 (Fed. Cir. 1991), **6.3, 7.9**

Semiconductor Energy Lab. Co. v. Samsung Elecs. Co., 204 F.3d 1368 (Fed. Cir. 2000), **10.2, 10.3**

Serrano v. Telular Corp., 111 F.3d 1578 (Fed. Cir. 1997), **7.12.2**

SIBIA Neurosciences, Inc. v. Cadus Pharm. Corp., 225 F.3d 1349 (Fed. Cir. 2000), **6.2, 9.8.1, 9.8.3, 9.8.4**

Singh v. Brake, 222 F.3d 1362 (Fed. Cir. 2000), **9.3.1, 9.3.9**

Slimfold Mfg. Co. v. Kinkead Indus., Inc., 932 F.2d 1453 (Fed. Cir. 1991), **11.6.2**

Smith & Nephew, Inc. v. Ethicon, Inc., 276 F.3d 1304 (Fed. Cir. 2001), **7.2, 7.4**

SmithKline Diagnostics, Inc. v. Helena Labs., Corp., 926 F.2d 1161 (Fed. Cir. 1991), **11.4, 11.5, 11.6.2**

Solomon v. Kimberly-Clark Corp., 216 F.3d 1372 (Fed. Cir. 2000), **9.1, 9.1.4**

Space Sys./Loral, Inc. v. Lockheed Martin Corp., 271 F.3d 1076 (Fed. Cir. 2001), **9.3.6**

Spectrum Int'l, Inc. v. Sterilite Corp., 164 F.3d 1372 (Fed. Cir. 1998), **6.5.1**

SRI Int'l, Inc. v. Advanced Tech. Labs., 127 F.3d 1462 (Fed. Cir. 1997), **8**

State Indus., Inc. v. Mor-Flo Indus., Inc., 883 F.2d 1573 (Fed. Cir. 1989), **11.4, 11.5, 11.6, 11.6.2, 11.9**

S3 Inc. v. nVIDIA Corp., 259 F.3d 1364 (Fed. Cir. 2001), **9.1.4**

Stiftung v. Renishaw, PLC, 945 F.2d 1173 (Fed. Cir. 1991), **6.5.1, 7.11**

Wang Lab. v. Toshiba Corp., 993 F.2d 858 (Fed. Cir. 1993), **9.8.1**

Warner-Jenkinson Co. v. Hilton Davis Chem. Co., 520 U.S. 17 (1997), **7.1, 7.3, 7.4, 7.8**

Water Techs. Corp. v. Calco, Ltd., 850 F.2d 660 (Fed. Cir. 1988), **11.4, 11.5**

Western Marine Elecs., Inc. v. Furuno Elec. Co., 764 F.2d 840 (Fed. Cir. 1985), **9.3.7**

Westvaco Corp. v. Int'l Paper Co., 991 F.2d 735 (Fed. Cir. 1993), **8**

Wilson Sporting Goods Co. v. David Geoffrey & Assocs., 904 F.2d 677 (Fed. Cir. 1990), **7.10**

Winner Int'l Royalty Corp. v. Wang, 202 F.3d 1340 (Fed. Cir. 2000), **9.8.2**

W.L. Gore & Assoc., Inc. v. Garlock, Inc., 721 F.2d 1540, *appeal after remand*, 842 F.2d 1275 (Fed. Cir. 1988), **9.1.4, 9.3.6, 9.6**

WMS Gaming, Inc. v. International Game Tech., 184 F.3d 1339 (Fed. Cir. 1999), **6.4, 7.5, 7.6, 8**

Wolverine World Wide, Inc. v. Nike, Inc., 38 F.3d 1192 (Fed. Cir. 1994), **6.2**

Woodland Trust v. Flowertree Nursery, Inc., 148 F.3d 1368 (Fed. Cir. 1998), **9.3.3, 9.3.4, 9.3.5**

Yamanouchi Pharm. Co. v. Danbury Pharmacal, Inc., 231 F.3d 1339 (Fed. Cir. 2000), **9.8, 9.8.2**

YBM Magnex, Inc. v. International Trade Comm'n, 145 F.3d 1317 (Fed. Cir. 1998), **7.4**

Zacharin v. United States, 213 F.3d 1366 (Fed. Cir. 2000), **9.3.6**

Zodiac Pool Care, Inc. v. Hoffinger Indus., Inc., 206 F.3d 1408 (Fed. Cir. 2000), **7.4**

Zygo Corp. v. Wyko Corp., 79 F.3d 1563 (Fed. Cir. 1996), **7.11, 11.4, 11.5, 11.6.2**

Index